A New Way to Buy a Car

-- 2nd Edition --

The Ultimate Consumer Awareness Guide for Novice & Experienced Car Shoppers

Gordon N. Wright, MBA

GORDON N. WRIGHT

CONTENTS

- The Importance of Value and Price
- The Steps to the Sale/Purchase
- Invoice Services and How to Use Them Wisely
- What Fees Must I Pay on a New Car?
- What is Digital Car Buying? Is it the Solution?

- Fuel Saving Technologies – A Short Primer on How to Not Be Confused
- Is it Time to Get Serious About an Electric Vehicle?
- Making Sense of the New Active Safety Technologies

DEDICATION

Dear Car Buyer/Shopper;

Choosing a new or used vehicle isn't easy. Why? Because you're bombarded with misleading advertising, confusing terminology, barely competent salespeople, and simply bad information from high-pressure sales to near worthless decision-making methods. How do you even find a qualified, competent professional car dealership or salesperson? **You start by reading this consumer guide**. In this fact-filled book based on my years of experience working directly with car shoppers in the car business, you'll <u>discover how to avoid the pitfalls</u> that trip up novice and experienced buyers alike. In this guide, you will discover:

- **Five Steps to a Hassle-Free Car Purchase**
- **Six Costly Misconceptions About Buying a Car**
- **Four Car Sales Rip-Offs to Avoid**
- **Ten Mistakes to Avoid When Visiting a Dealership**
- **How to Get Maximum Dollars for Your Trade-in**
- **How to Win the Battle with the Business Manager**
- **The Decision to Lease or Buy**
- **Understanding the Car Buying Process**
- **Understanding the New Technologies Facing Car Buyers**

Soon after entering the car business more than a decade ago, I realized that knowledgeable and informed buyers were the easiest to work with and were more willing to get right to the point. They were the folks who appreciated a relationship that was based on mutual respect. So, I eventually wrote a guide to help all of you <u>better understand car buying</u> and <u>how to navigate the process for a better car buying experience</u>. Now, with the information provided in this consumer guide, you can make an informed, intelligent decision and avoid the most common pitfalls.

This **2nd Edition** includes new topics that were barely on the horizon when I wrote the first consumer guide. Plus, the rest of the book has been re-written to capture other changes in products and technology since 2015. Although the retail automotive scene has improved somewhat with the power of the internet, social media, and the instant access to information that smartphones have allowed, much of the industry continues to be stuck in outdated methods and organization structures that reward manipulation and shady business practices. My hope is that this consumer awareness guide will help to level the playing field as you set out to acquire your next car, truck or SUV.

Cordially,

Gordon Wright,
A Friend in the Car Business
www.AFriendintheCarBusiness.com

ACKNOWLEDGEMENTS

Thanks to the increasing number of car sales professionals who are not pressured by "old school" Sales Managers into employing the tactics and manipulations that this book is meant to overcome. This small but growing number of salespeople gives me the hope and inspiration that the retail car business will continue to move into the 21st Century and leave the methods of the past behind. Most car manufacturers are now pushing dealers in this direction by increasing the incentives for delivering first class purchase experiences and imposing penalties for substandard performance. But, until this trend overtakes the industry, consumers must continue to be alert and ready to deal with the minority of bad apples still plying their trade at dealerships across the country.

This book will help you find those enlightened salespeople and Sales Managers who are dedicated to serving customers in an open and transparent fashion and it will also help you to spot and deal with those who are still working with attitudes and approaches from an earlier century. Buying a car should be fun and can be an enjoyable experience if you keep your wits about you and use the information in this book to locate car sales professionals who are interested in **creating customers for life**.

FOREWORD

Some Car Buying Ground Rules

The Traditional Car Buying Process will be around for some time and you will be dealing with human beings on the sales side whose earnings are directly or indirectly tied to convincing you to buy or lease a vehicle today. This book provides a new way to approach the traditional car buying process now that you (the buyer) have new tools and technologies available to you that can level the playing field.

There are also a number of new car purchase models emerging that I call the Vending Machine Car Acquisition Process (sometimes referred to as Digital or Online Vehicle Purchase) where most of the human contact is taken out of the equation and it becomes a mechanical, transactional process. Technology is making it possible to complete all elements of the purchase process online. For those who are serial car buyers and consider a car to be an appliance, there is some appeal to this acquisition model. It is essentially the "Amazon" model and it will likely represent a portion of the market in the future. In this guide, we will consider this model but the bulk of the book is concerned with the more traditional car buying process where most of the retail car industry operates.

As technology evolves, you may or may not end up owning a vehicle in the traditional sense of the word. The "sharing economy" is changing a lot of the rules about car ownership. You might just end up "borrowing" a vehicle (or collection of vehicles) in the near future. In fact, those options are already available for some vehicles and in some locations. Nevertheless, virtually all of us need to find at least one or more transportation solutions to address our requirement to get places for work, play, or simple social interaction.

This guide will focus on navigating the traditional car buying process, however, it will also introduce you to the new car selling methods often associated with <u>new car selling technologies</u> that you may encounter. As vehicles become more complicated and sophisticated and the range of "ownership" options expands dramatically, even experienced car buyers will find themselves in unfamiliar territory. Remember when your only options were to buy or lease? With sharing, fractional ownership, rental arrangements, and subscription methods of car ownership now emerging on the scene, the whole process can become a bit confusing. These "ownership" methods are not for everyone but the market for transportation services is getting fragmented and the lines are blurring between private ownership, sharing, and public transportation systems.

You now also have a choice of the type of vehicle you select. Should you be considering an EV (electric vehicle) or a hybrid, or diesel, or a traditional gasoline internal combustion engine? We will consider how to sort out these choices as well as how to make sense of the quickly evolving safety and collision-avoidance technologies now becoming standard on even entry-level vehicles.

How to Read This Book

<u>Note</u>, you can **read this book in any order**. The <u>first four chapters</u> cover the most popular car buying tips and nuggets of advice I have provided to my own customers. The topics selected are based on the traffic and comments from my original postings in a blog called, *"A Friend in the Car Business"*. The balance of the book covers <u>the most important topics I believe you need to understand</u> to be truly successful in your car purchase project. This latter portion of the book also deals with how the car buying process and the vehicles themselves have changed over the past few years and why that is important. Enjoy the ride!

Chapter 1

FIVE STEPS TO A HASSLE-FREE CAR PURCHASE

It really is possible to turn a potentially scary and frustrating endeavor into an easy and pleasant experience as long as you follow the advice in this guide. Car dealerships and car salespeople want the process to go smoothly as well, however, this is most likely to happen when the car purchaser (i.e., you) is familiar with how the process works and approaches the project with knowledge and confidence. This guide will help you do that. Let's get started.....

Step #1 - Know What You Want/Need

Separating what you need from what you want can be the most difficult part of the car buying experience so, if you do not have these two issues clear in your head before you venture out to the Auto Mall, you are likely to become frustrated and/or be taken advantage of by shrewd car salespeople.

1

Here's an exercise to help you sort out what kind of vehicle makes the most sense given your current transportation situation and future plans. Answer the questions and then check the recommendations:

How many people will be in the car most of the time? If, for 90% of the time and mileage, it is only you and possibly one other person in the car, then a small, fuel-efficient car may be all you need and a subcompact or compact car will fit the bill. If you expect half a dozen out-of-town family or friends to visit from time to time, consider renting a van for those weekends rather than buying a bigger car that you don't really need on a daily basis. Even most subcompact cars will seat four people comfortably. (If you are above average in height and/or weight, the sub-compact option may not work for you). Of course, if you are frequently transporting several people and/or cargo, a family- size sedan, **Sport Utility Vehicle** (SUV), or minivan might better suit your requirements.

What kind of activities will the vehicle be required to address? For example, if you are an outdoor enthusiast who is headed to the ski hills every weekend during the winter, you may decide that All-Wheel-Drive would be worth having on your next vehicle to handle that deep snow or the unpredictable weather you will frequently encounter. If it's mainly a commuter car, the comments about the number of people normally in the car will give you the answer. If you are a home improvement enthusiast, those trips to your local building center for 2x4's and wood panels will go a lot better with a van or SUV or even a truck. And for young families, a minivan is hard to beat when you need to be getting your children and a few of their friends to the soccer game or hockey rink (along with their equipment). Make sure that the new vehicle lines up with your lifestyle and fits within an overall transportation plan.

Does the vehicle mix in your driveway make sense? If you have (or need) two or more vehicles to accommodate the number of drivers in the family, think about what combination of vehicle types will provide the best mix. One large family vehicle and one small commuter vehicle might be the optimum way to cover the "number of people normally in the car" issue as well as the kinds of activities for which the vehicles will be needed. Also, the age and life expectancy of the vehicles in the driveway will help determine which vehicle is now the one to be replaced and what kind of vehicle/driver reassignment would make the most sense. There is no right or wrong answer, however, these should be among your considerations.

What makes sense for your family life cycle stage? Every five to seven years, you will find that the family needs change as children grow and leave home and your transportation needs (or wants) change. Have a plan that sees you rotating your "fleet" of vehicles so you do not have all the vehicles in your driveway aging and coming due for replacement at the same time. If you can replace vehicles before they lose all their value, you will also lower maintenance costs and put yourself in a position to get that two-seater sports car before you are too old to enjoy it.

Step #2 - Know What You Can Afford

As I stress elsewhere in this book, most successful car buyers have developed a budget before getting very far into the car purchase process and you should too. Here's a simple way to understand **what you can afford based on how the banks determine what you can afford**. This is important because the banks will be determining how much they are willing to lend you based on your credit score (covered later in this section) and your specific financial circumstances. Let's draft a budget that the banks will be receptive to approving.

Step 1. **Your Gross Income x 15% = Maximum Car Payment**. If your gross income (before taxes and other deductions) is $5,000 per month, your car payment should be under 15% of gross income (15%

x $5,000 =) $750 per month. Use your own pay slip to substitute the $5,000 with your gross income before taxes have been deducted.

Step 2. The bank is also concerned about your ability to pay back the loan so they want to know what other debt obligations you already have to manage. The banks call this your TDSR (Total Debt Service Ratio). If the total of your car loan payment + credit card payment + rent/mortgage payments is too high, the banks become less willing to lend. A safe TDSR is about 35%. That means your car loan payment + credit card payment + rent/mortgage payments should be under 35% of gross income (35% x $5,000 =) $1,750.

Your Gross Income x 35% = Maximum Debt Service (Payments). Of course, in this example, if your rent and credit card (or other loan) payments total $1,400 it means **your car payment cannot exceed $350** ($1,750 less $1,200 rent less $200 other debt payments). Foe most of us who have rent (or a mortgage) to pay along with other credit obligations, this Maximum Debt Service calculation is the one the banks will be most concerned about.

If your financial affairs are in great shape (as reflected by your Credit Score), you become an attractive customer that the banks desire. This means that the above ratios become more flexible. You may even be approved for your car loan based only on your credit score meaning you may not be required to provide detailed income and employment information.

In order to maintain a healthy credit score, follow these rules:

Avoid missing payments on any loans or regular financial obligations

Don't carry a balance (if possible). Pay off the credit card balance each month or certainly do not carry it over for more than a month or two. Always make a monthly payment.

Keep loan applications to a minimum. No "shotgunning" to see where you can get approved. That means, do not work multiple car deals at different dealers to see where you get the best rate or the best deal.

Credit bureaus view this kind of activity as a "red flag" that you are having trouble getting approved by several banks.

Maintain a Good Credit Score. Here's what the numbers mean:

760 or above. Excellent. You will easily qualify for the best available rates.

725-759. Very Good. You will likely get approved at the lowest available rate.

660-724. Good. You should not have trouble getting approved but it may not be at the lowest possible rate.

560-659. Fair. Once you slip into the Fair category, you should not have trouble getting approved but it gets very difficult to get approved for the low interest rate loans.

300-559. Poor. If you are in this group, the only option is a low with a high interest rate.

Regardless of what the banks consider safe, you want to be sure you are feeling confident that you are not taking on an obligation you cannot handle. So before you head to your local car dealership with that newspaper ad that shouts out that you can own that shiny new (insert your favorite car brand) for as little as $199 a month, take a step back and think of all the costs involved in car ownership (particularly if this is your first car). Also those ads that make just about any car appear affordable are usually talking about a base-level vehicle and/or are assuming a hefty down payment which you might not have available.

In a finance or lease scenario, you will have car payments plus insurance premiums, and gas and maintenance costs (although the latter will be minimal during the first few years when you are covered by the manufacturer's comprehensive warranty). The best approach is to estimate all your monthly expenses grouping them by **Fixed** (rent, utilities, insurance, cable TV, etc.) and **Variable** (food, clothing, entertainment, etc.). If you have been keeping track of these expenses, this exercise is much easier. Plug in your new transportation costs based on what you can afford including <u>insurance</u>. Your automobile insurance agent will be happy to quote you on the cost to insure a specific Year, Make and Model of vehicle. Now you are ready to select a dealership and a car sales professional to work with.

Step #3 - Find a Dealer You Can Trust

Despite the sophisticated information technology now available to put the buyer in the driver's seat, buying a car is still a major decision with a big emotional component. Plus, to complete the vehicle selection and find the right financing package means you are likely going to be visiting the dealership and interacting with a car salesperson or product advisor. (A lot of people find that, alone, a scary prospect and that's why I will recommend, later in this book, that you introduce yourself to the Sales Manager or Internet Manager). It is becoming easier to do the entire process via phone and email so you can avoid coming into the dealership for anything other than signing the final purchase documents (and even that is changing as new digital platforms are rolled out). However, this works best for a segment of the population who has bought vehicles in the past and knows exactly what they want. For most shoppers, it will not guarantee that you get the right car.

The truth is that, with the odd exception, most people end up making a final decision on which car to buy and how they are going to pay for it <u>when they are at the dealership</u> and have found a salesperson who is helpful and trustworthy. But this doesn't mean you can't use the internet to make the process easier and less stressful. With the internet, you can **"audition" your prospective salesperson** before you go to the dealership.

Some internet shoppers seem to overlook the opportunity to use the internet to seek out a competent and professional salesperson. Instead, they use the net to try and negotiate a final price via email. This simply encourages the less than professional salespeople out there to use various tricks to get you into the dealership. Use the internet and the phone to find a person you can trust.

At most dealerships, internet inquiries are handled by a senior salesperson or by the Sales Manager. Once you receive a reply to your internet or email query, find out if this is someone you want to do business with. When you send in a quote/information request, you should get a very prompt response. Many people send requests to multiple dealers in their area. Here's your chance to gauge the responses. Who was quickest to respond? Who provided a bit more information or a few alternative suggestions? Who sent you a personalized response versus an automated response? If you provided a phone number, you should expect a call. Are you getting straight answers to your questions or are you finding the dealership person to be evasive?

Because very few people actually buy a car over the phone or internet, dealership salespeople will want you to visit the dealership. Use your email and phone conversations to **determine who is the most deserving of your business before making an appointment**. Once you feel you have someone at the other end of the line who is committed to helping you, book an appointment and arrive prepared with the questions that you are most keen to have answered and an idea of what features the "perfect vehicle" will have. If you have multiple vehicles in your household or you are "upside down" on a lease that you need to get out of, let the salesperson know your situation and ask for alternatives for you to consider.

Sometimes new technology just makes life more complicated. Use the power of the internet to simplify the car buying process and get connected to a car salesperson who will act as your adviser instead of an adversary. With the digital tools available, it is not difficult to research and read reviews about competing dealerships and specific salespeople. Make sure you spend some of your time "shopping for a salesperson and dealership" once you have selected a short list of vehicles. Find a friend in the car business and enjoy the car buying process as much as you plan to enjoy your new car.

Step #4 - Understand How You are Vulnerable in the Business Office

You may doubt that the person you will meet in the Business Office will be the unscrupulous character you've been warned about as you researched the car buying process. You may even think that these kinds of characters must be part of a past era in car shopping. Modern dealerships must be more enlightened than the stories circulating online. But, these people don't get their reputation from a few random rogues in the business. They get their reputation from what a majority of them do, from what they are trained to do, from what they are expected to do by their owners. So before you enter the Business Office (Finance Office), please be clear that **the person you will meet has only one job and that is to make profit for the dealership**. They will normally do anything and say anything to achieve that objective.

You can be sure that the Business Manager will employ every sales trick and technique available because they know you are at your most vulnerable point in the car buying process. The successful Business Manager understands buyer psychology. They don't need a PhD because they have already proven to the dealership principal than they can quickly and efficiently size up a client and (with the help of the salesperson who has planted a few seeds during the sales process) determine your hot buttons.

Once you have purchased the vehicle, your guard is down and you will be assured that the next part of the process is easy. But the Business Manager knows that **when we cross the line from being a car shopper to a car owner, our mindset undergoes a change**. Now, it is <u>our car</u> (not the dealer's car). Our relationship to the car and to the dealership has changed. Now we are a customer (in our minds) but still a prospect to the Business Manager who has products yet to sell us.

At the same time, the Business Manager understands that another psychological barrier has been crossed that is called, in the auto industry, **"Second Money"**. The "First Money" was your agreement to purchase the vehicle at a specific price or payment. "Second Money" refers to the fact that once that hurdle has been achieved, you are more susceptible to a request for more money. You see, your brain becomes excited and energized by the idea of crossing the line to ownership and you are open to stoking that fire by purchasing something else, especially if presented with a well crafted sales pitch. You can probably think back to shopping excursions for clothing or technology or household goods where you experienced the same phenomenon. Not only did you buy the suit, you left the store with shirts, ties and a belt that were not part of your purchase plan that day.

It is hard to overstate the power of these psychological pressures that we are hardly aware of or understand. Nevertheless, they are acting on us and they present real opportunities in the hands of a skilled sales professional. And the Business Manager gets paid the big bucks (from your pocket) because he/she is normally the most skilled sales pro at the dealership. <u>Be sure to read Chapter 6</u> that gets into specific actions you can take to come out ahead when dealing with the Business Manager.

Step #5 - Read and Understand the Purchase Agreement

If you purchase a new or used vehicle, you will need to sign a Vehicle Purchase Agreement to make the deal binding. Despite the fact that the following notice is provided in bold type right above the purchaser's signature on all contracts signed in Ontario, many car buyers sign without fully understanding the commitment they are making. In most jurisdictions, you will find similar "fine print" on your Purchase Agreement or Bill of Sale. Here is what the note says (in Ontario) and what you are agreeing to when you sign the agreement:

ALL SALES FINAL. Please review the entire Agreement, including all attached statements, before signing. This Agreement is final and binding once you have signed it unless the motor vehicle dealer has failed to comply with certain legal obligations.

In most jurisdictions, there is no "cooling off" period when purchasing a motor vehicle. (See the Car Buying Resources section - Chapter 11 - at the end of the book for a list of jurisdictions with variations to the no-cooling-off period). If you want to cancel a vehicle purchase agreement, the dealer is entitled to claim "liquidated damages" and retain a portion, or all, of your deposit. In practice, most dealerships will make every effort to accommodate reasonable requests from buyers even after the deal is done, however, there is no legal obligation to do so. Some of the obvious things you should check before signing involve the vehicle you are purchasing and the accessories and add-ons included in the deal:

- Are all the accessories you ordered clearly showing? If the salesperson mentioned throwing in free oil changes for a year or an iPod to close the deal, make sure they are listed on the agreement, otherwise, everyone's memory will become suddenly cloudy when you come to pick up the car and ask about those extras.

- <u>Is the model code showing and color code indicated</u>? It doesn't happen often, but it is not uncommon for a customer to "think" they were buying a specific trim level but a different trim level and/or color was put on the agreement. When this happens, (in my experience) it's seldom malicious, however mistakes happen. If you ordered a vehicle with that technology package, make sure it appears on the agreement.

- <u>Are you paying for things you never discussed</u>? If you find "doc" fees, administration charges, security packages, or other charges you don't understand, be sure you get an explanation before you sign. This is a favorite area to bury extra charges with the hope that you don't notice.

Don't Forget to Read the Back. On the back of the agreement are several statements that you are also agreeing to comply with. For example, the dealer has 90 days to deliver your car. No matter what the salesperson said about it only taking a few days or a week to get the car for you, the dealership can delay delivery for a number of reasons. (Or, they may have trouble getting the exact trim/color you ordered in a timely fashion). Unless it is written into the agreement, there is no obligation by the dealer to provide you with a loaner car or free rental if your vehicle is delayed for any reason. I have seen vehicles delayed for lots of reasons including labor stoppages at the port, difficulty getting another dealer to transfer a vehicle, and even transportation companies "misplacing" the vehicle in transit (to name a few). Believe me, the dealer wants to deliver a sold vehicle as quickly as possible because no one at the dealership gets paid until the vehicle is delivered.

Trade-in Disclosures. The laws and regulations vary by state and province but where I operate, in Ontario Canada, the Ontario Motor Vehicle Act requires that the seller of any used car completely disclose all relevant information on the vehicle being sold. This applies whether you are a dealer or a private citizen. If you have a trade-in, you are selling your old car to the dealership. If you fail to disclose a material fact about your old car, you may be liable to future owners of that vehicle. That's why the dealer taking in your trade will ask you to sign a series of disclosures about your trade-in. Be sure to disclose all relevant facts (such as previous damage exceeding $3,000, etc.) before handing over your keys.

One Last Comment. I have seen lots of people shopping for a new car traveling from dealer to dealer while considering several makes/models before working out a final deal at a dealership. The danger in "over shopping" is that when you finally decide on a vehicle, you may have assumed something in the deal that was part of a discussion at another dealership. Or, you test drove a GT model and ended up settling on a GS model (which is missing a couple of features important to you). Because I have seen this happen, I recommend reviewing the fine print before signing and before making your final commitment. **If it is not documented in the purchase agreement, it is not legally part of the deal.**

Chapter 2

SIX COSTLY MISCONCEPTIONS ABOUT BUYING A CAR

Misconception #1 - The Best Deals are Only Available at Certain Times

If asked, "When is the best time to buy a new car?", most people would probably answer the question by saying **"the end of the model year"** for the vehicle you have in mind. The rationale, of course, is that no manufacturer or dealer wants to have the old model year inventory once the new vehicles have arrived and they are willing to cut a deal to clear the remaining prior model year vehicles. That's normally what I tell customers as well, however, <u>when is the end of the model year</u>? It turns out that any month could be the end of the model year. In the "old days", September was the month that the new models arrived (especially on American car dealers' lots). And that is

13

probably why August is still one of the highest sales months for most dealerships. But now, with production cycles staggered to minimize downtime and cars being shipped from Europe, Japan, and all over North America, new models may start arriving as early as July and as late as December. And, if the new model year vehicle has undergone a major styling update, manufacturers are now frequently launching the new vehicles during the first quarter (January through March).

When you buy at the end of the model year, you are often foregoing the opportunity to get the latest technology that is coming on the new vehicle. For example, the National Highway Traffic Safety Administration and Transport Canada have both issued regulations requiring that all new passenger cars and SUVs must be equipped with **"rear-view visibility systems".** If you saved some money on your 2017 Model Year purchase that does not have a backup camera, you may find that the trade-in value in a couple of years is significantly lower because you missed getting this important safety feature.

With an increasingly competitive marketplace, car manufacturers have had to become smarter about matching supply and demand. Rather than building cars "just in case" customers came in to buy, the new paradigm is to build the cars "just in time". This means that during the Model Year, manufacturers are monitoring the inventory in the pipeline on a monthly basis and adjusting production, promotions, and incentives (specifically by model). The objective is to be selling the last few vehicles from the current Model Year when the new Model Year vehicles start to arrive. The manufacturers and their dealers are getting very good at this balancing act. The system is not perfect but the truth about Model Year clearance events is that you can usually get a deal but it often is not on the color or trim level that you want. And, I have seen customers deciding to wait for a few more weeks to get a better deal only to find that the model they want is sold out when they come back.

If you have your eye on a particular brand/model and you have the flexibility to wait for the end of the model year, make sure you do the following to maximize your savings:

- *Find out when the new Model Year vehicles are starting to arrive.* This is normally the point where both the selection and the incentives on the outgoing Model Year vehicles are at or near their max. You can find out by simply calling your local dealership and saying you are interested in the new Model Year vehicles and ask when they will start arriving. That's the point at which you will want to check out the remaining inventory and year end incentives on the outgoing Model Year vehicles.

- *Do the final deal near the end of the month.* High volume dealers who are trying to hit volume targets for that month are often more willing to cut a real deal just to hit a volume target and if you schedule the delivery for early the following month, you may be able to get the dealer to "protect" the deal in case the manufacturer boosts the incentives for the following month.

- *Consider paying cash.* Sometimes, the cash incentives are better than the finance incentives. Also, your best payment on a specific car may be found by negotiating the cash price and financing the car at the preferred dealership finance rate. Consider both options before buying.

Misconception #2 - To Save Money, Look for 0% Interest

In recent years, the use of low financing rates by auto manufacturers as an incentive to purchase a new car has "progressed" to the point where there is an expectation that 0% financing will be available on any and all vehicles in the dealer's showroom. I have even had customers come into the store and ask if we had 0% financing (before finding out if we had the type of vehicle that might fit their needs). Because everyone has now been conditioned to accept nothing other than 0% financing, they are often <u>missing an opportunity to save money</u>.

Let me explain. Toward the end of the Model Year for a vehicle, the 0% financing incentives often get extended to 72 or 84 months so that the outgoing model year vehicles get moved off the lot as the new model year vehicles arrive. **The car manufacturers use their marketing funds to buy down the finance rates to these very attractive levels**. When you buy a car under these 0% terms, you normally forego the option to pay cash (which may mean passing up a significant rebate or discount off the price). With a cash purchase, the car manufacturer "saves" the marketing funds that would have been used to reduce the rate to 0% and provides **a cash rebate/discount**. But, did you know that <u>you can take the cash discount and still finance the car</u>? Yes you can and you might just save money that way.

With most car brands, you can take the "discount for cash" and still **finance the vehicle at the <u>standard rate</u>** (which is the preferred rate that the manufacturer has negotiated with the bank). For example, let's consider a typical compact SUV situation where an outgoing model year vehicle can be financed for <u>60 months at 0%</u> **OR** you can take a <u>$4,500 cash discount and finance it at 4.99%</u> for the same period. Which option would you choose? Check out the table below:

Purchase Options	0% Option	Cash w/4.99%
Vehicle MSRP*	$23,195	$23,195
Freight, PDE, Fees**	$2,025	$2,025
Mfgr. Discount for Cash	$0	($4,500)
Cost of the Vehicle	$25,220	$20,720

Sales Tax @ 13%	$3,279	$2,694
Amount to Finance	$28,499	$23,414
Cost of Financing	$0	$3,090
Total Amount Paid	**$28,499**	**$26,504**
Monthly Payment	$475	$442

*MSRP = Manufacturer's Suggested Retail Price
**PDE = Pre-Delivery Expense

It turns out **you save $1,995** over 60 months <u>if you choose the **Cash Discount option**</u>. So, **you are not saving money (in this case) by opting for the 0% financing**. You are paying more! And, another benefit, if you pay off the loan early, you save some of the interest that is not possible on the 0% option.

Effectively, <u>there are two prices for this vehicle</u>. You need to calculate which program works best for you. Depending on the "standard finance rate" and the amount of the "discount for cash" on the vehicle you are considering, it may be to your advantage to opt for the Cash Purchase option even though you are not financing it at 0%. <u>Always consider both options</u>.

Misconception #3- Asking Several Dealers for Their "Best Price" Gets the Best Deal

Most, if not all, car buyers now use the internet to do preliminary research when considering a car purchase, which is great because an informed buyer is a better buyer. Even most car salespeople would agree with this statement. However, some car buyers then decide on a specific Make/Model and use the internet to get competing dealers to bid on the selected vehicle. This car shopping approach seems simple and logical but it can complicate the process as well as lead to disappointment and I'll tell you why.

If it were not for something called Human Nature, getting several Honda dealers (for example) in your area to bid on supplying you with a specific Honda Civic (substitute the Make/Model of your choice) would seem to be a simple way to get the best price. What could go wrong? Every dealer is just going to provide their best price and hope you choose them, right? Not quite!

If you ask competing dealers to bid on supplying a specific car, they all want to get the business and they all want to do it at a profit (or at worst, breakeven). Now, leaving the possibility of outright dishonesty aside, every bidding dealer has an incentive (in this situation) to structure the bid so it **appears to be the lowest**. They can do this by:

- Quoting a "cash purchase" price instead of a low interest finance price

- Leaving out certain fees, taxes, and levies

- Assuming in the quote that certain fees will be paid upfront and only the balance is used to calculate the monthly finance payment

- Quoting a payment based on a longer term than requested

- Quoting on a slightly different version of the vehicle than requested (or understood)

- Assuming some rebates for which you may not qualify (e.g. first time buyer, student, loyalty program, etc.)

So, you send out your request for quotation to several Honda dealers (to stay with the example above) and you get back various numbers and different levels of detail. If all the dealers are acting ethically and your specifications are very detailed, there should not be more than a couple of hundred dollars difference between the highest quote and the lowest quote. Now what do you do? In the final analysis, this is likely to be the case if every dealer is quoting on the same assumptions because dealer margins on popular car makes/models are only 6% to 8%.

A more likely scenario is that you will get one or two quotes that appear to be a couple of thousand dollars lower than the rest. Now what do you do? Clearly, two dealers selling the same car under the same terms in an extremely competitive market cannot be off by a few thousand dollars. The only explanation is that the low-ball bidder (and usually that's just what it is) has provided a **phony number** (using one of the above assumptions) in order to get you into the dealership. If you get a bid like this, it is a red flag that something fishy is going on.

All dealers in Ontario (as in most jurisdictions) know that you can only legally purchase a motor vehicle by presenting yourself at the dealership and signing a purchase agreement on the premises. Therefore, dealers will do their utmost to get you in the store with the assumption that they can close the sale on terms that favor the dealership. That's why it is a recipe for confusion and frustration to send out requests for quotation when there are other means available to determine a fair price without going through a blizzard of back and forth emails to numerous dealerships to "clarify" the bids and still not be sure once you select a "winning bidder".

To help determine a fair price, there are a number of services available such as **Unhaggle.com** and **CarCostCanada.com** in Canada that will provide the dealer's net invoice cost on a vehicle along with current rebates and incentives. In the US, you can use **TrueCar.com** or **Edmunds.com** (both of which have a "true market value" tool that provides average amounts paid in your region by Make, Model, and Trim level), however, manufacturers in the US have been reluctant to provide data to third parties that will find its way to consumers. In Canada, the market is structured somewhat differently and it is easier for consumers to access the dealer's invoice price, however, the holdbacks and similar direct-to-dealer incentives are different for each manufacturer and are never made public.

Misconception #4 - Aggressive Negotiating Will Get You the Best Deal

I always suggest that car buyers negotiate **after** buying the car! I know that sounds illogical at first glance, but hear me out. Often, customers (mistakenly) spend a lot of time and emotional energy negotiating a discount on the price of the vehicle only to **overpay** for protection packages and other add-ons (such as tinted windows, rustproofing, accessories, etc.) when they are signing the paperwork in the **Business Office**. It is my contention that you are actually better off to pay closer to the sticker price on the car and then negotiate vigorously on the extras (many of which are worth having and help to hold the value of the car but are almost always overpriced).

Now there is nothing wrong with negotiating with the dealer to save some money on the price of the car. But, most customers who are set on saving money on their purchase (or fear that they will be ripped off if they don't play hard ball) are so satisfied with themselves after hammering the dealer for a significant discount that they let down their defenses when they sit down with the business manager. That's where the dealer makes most of the profit on the overall sale. Now that you "own" the car and you have saved money on the purchase, you are more susceptible to a skillful sales pitch on protecting your investment with rust proofing, additional warranty protection, or other add-ons.

The car business is not unlike other big ticket retail products in that the percentage margin that the retailer makes on a flat screen TV or SLR camera is small compared to what they make on the camera case or added warranty package. <u>Edmunds.com</u> (USA data) recently listed the gross margin on the most popular compact cars:

- Toyota Corolla   6.5%
- Ford Focus   5.5%
- Honda Civic   7.8%
- Hyundai Elantra   2.7%
- Mazda3   6.2%

If you consider that Walmart (the king of discount retailing) makes an average gross margin of 25% and Costco makes about 15%, the margins being made on popularly priced new cars are pretty thin. Consider also that there are over 25 compact car brands competing for the available business so there is not much room for car companies to hide thousands of dollars of margin and still be competitive. For cars that are built outside North America, it is even tougher as these cars must pay the 6.1% non-NAFTA tariff and still price themselves against locally built vehicles.

You might ask, how can dealerships survive on these thin margins? The answer is, they don't. Dealerships make their money on <u>used cars</u>, the <u>service and parts department</u>, and the <u>additional products and services</u> you buy once you have committed to purchase your new car, i.e., rust protection packages, extended warranties, tinted windows, dealer installed accessories, and other add-ons. Dealers also get rebates from the manufacturer for hitting volume targets and achieving customer service targets at the end of the year.

But might want to save the hard bargaining for the Business Office where their aim is to recover whatever was lost up front and then some.

Misconception #5 - Using Your Line-of-Credit is a Good Idea

There are a lot of prudent ways to use a Line-of-Credit but using it to buy a car is probably not one of them. One of the dangers of putting an automobile on a Line-of-Credit is that if you miss a payment, the bank can simply deduct the money from your savings or chequing account. Or, in a worst-case scenario, foreclose on your house if it is a Home Equity Line-of- Credit.

A more rational reason for not using a Line-of-Credit is the unstructured nature of the loan. It's what I call the "**Never Ever Loan**" because <u>it never ever seems to get paid off</u>. Once you have put a few purchases on your Line-of-Credit, you start to lose track of whether the car is anywhere near being paid off. With a proper car loan, you know where you are at any point and you will eventually get it paid off. If you miss payments on a structured car loan, the worst that can happen is that the car gets repossessed (not your home).

Some people are tempted to use their Line-of-Credit because the **variable rate** they are getting is lower than the **fixed rate** available through the dealer (particularly on used cars). But a variable rate is just that...<u>variable</u>. Therefore, a fixed rate that is guaranteed for the full term of the loan and is fully open (to be paid off without penalty) is the preferred method of financing your new or used car.

If you are <u>buying a used car</u> that's less that five years old, the car loan you get through the dealer will likely be better than what your bank can provide to you directly. That's because the major banks have a huge dealer lending program that sees rates that can be as low as 3.9% to 6.9%. On older cars (and for weaker borrowers), rates are double or triple these levels. Right now, because pre-owned vehicles are a stronger focus at most dealerships, car manufacturers and financial institutions have come up with much sharper pricing of rates for used cars than in the past. Remember, if you are quoted a finance rate on a used car by your dealer, **the rate is negotiable** if your credit is good. Also remember that loans under $10,000 carry the highest rates.

If you are <u>buying a new car</u>, very low (or 0%) finance rates are available for credit worthy buyers. These rates are subsidized by the car manufacturer to help the dealership sell cars. You may find that the rates are so low on a new car purchase that the monthly payments for a new car are very similar to those for a used car because the interest cost difference is greater than the list price difference. That's why it may make sense to pay cash for a used car (if you have the cash) but finance a new car.

Misconception #6 - Selling Your Current Vehicle Yourself is Better Than Trading It In

When it comes time to retire your vehicle, you have a decision to make regarding what to do with the old car that is no longer meeting your needs. You essentially have 4 options: You can **KEEP IT, GIVE IT AWAY, SELL IT YOURSELF, or SELL IT TO THE DEALER**.

You may have your own reasons for <u>keeping it</u> or <u>giving it away</u>. As a car sales professional, I cannot help with those two options except to advise you in general terms. Usually these two alternatives are the same because if you keep an old car, it is frequently done in order to give it to a family member.

Now the question is: **Are you planning to <u>sell it yourself</u> or <u>sell it to the dealer</u>**?

If You Sell It Yourself, You Need Two Things: <u>Time & Money</u>

You Also Need to:

- Find Parking Space
- Keep it Insured
- Clean & Detail It
- Re-condition It (Repair what is not working)
- Advertise It
- Show It (including Booking Appointments & Road Tests)
- Get an M.T.O. Used Car Package (in Ontario)
- Provide a Bill of Sale
- Provide a CarProof (or CarFax) Vehicle History Report
- Collect Cash/Certified Funds
- Forego the Sales Tax Benefit

If You Sell It To The Dealer: You Enjoy these Benefits and Avoid some Risks

- The Dealer Pays Fair Value for your "as-is" Condition Vehicle
- The Dealer takes on the Time and Risk of Selling Your Vehicle
- You Simply Drop off Your Old Vehicle and Drive Away in Your New Vehicle.
- If you are trading in your old vehicle, you only pay tax on the difference between the new car price and the value of your trade. This taxable saving will often cover most of the difference in the retail value of your trade-in vehicle.

The popular belief is that you can get more money by putting a "For Sale" sign on your car or paying for online advertising and selling it yourself than if you trade it in at a dealer. Many people hold that belief because they see values for similar vehicles online that are higher than what the dealer is offering.

Most dealers should be able to get you the Black Book (wholesale) price for your "as-is" vehicle which will be lower than the retail asking prices you will find on **autoTRADER** and similar sites. Typically, prices appearing online from private sellers and dealerships are not the prices that the vehicles eventually sell at. As well, dealers selling used cars are normally including some safety certification, warranty, and special financing.

A frequent scenario that I have run into with trade-in vehicles is a customer who has a trade-in offer from me (the dealership) and has a buyer (more or less lined up) who is willing to pay more but wants the vehicle safety certified. During the safety certification process, the mechanic discovers a mechanical problem that must be repaired. Once all the costs of getting the vehicle certified are calculated, there is often very little difference from the offer received from the dealer.

I always suggest to customers that if they are in such a quandary, they can **go with the firm offer from the dealer** (as their fall back position) and continue to try and sell their trade-in vehicle until it is time to take delivery of their new car. If they do better privately in the meantime, they can pocket the difference. It's a win/win.

Chapter 3

FOUR CAR SALES RIP-OFFS TO AVOID

Rip-Off #1 - Rustproofing

As someone who has personally purchased rustproofing on most of the vehicles I have ever owned, I am not suggesting that you not buy rustproofing for your new car, however, <u>paying too much for rustproofing is where the rip-off usually occurs</u>. As I explain elsewhere in this guide, you should <u>be prepared to negotiate</u> on any after-purchase products and services but you need to know what is reasonable.

Once you have purchased the vehicle and you are sitting in the Business Manager's office getting the final paperwork completed and banking arrangements sorted out, you will be offered the opportunity to "<u>protect</u>" your vehicle by getting one or more of the following done: **rustproofing**, **undercoating**, **fabric protection**, and **paint protection**. Often, these are packaged together. Usually these extras are sold as "just two or three more dollars on your biweekly payment". Find out what the total amount will be and ask yourself if it makes sense. Dealers often get away with selling these packages for thousands of dollars when you really should be paying hundreds.

The two rust protection methods available are <u>Spray Protection</u> and <u>Electronic Module Protection</u>. Here's how they compare and work:

1. **Spray.** Best done when the car is new, this approach involves spraying various substances on the underside of the vehicle as well as inside rocker panels, the hood, trunk, doors and wheel wells to coat surfaces. The purpose is to prevent moisture and road chemicals, such as salt, from interacting with the metal. These are three basic methods:

    a. <u>Oil-Based</u> is applied annually and is good at working its way into the many crevices where rust can potentially get started. The major provider of this treatment is **Krown**. This is the method recommended by the <u>Automobile Protection Association</u>. Oil-based products have a tendency to drip for several days after application and must be re-applied (usually annually) to maintain the protective effect.

    b. <u>Silicone Based</u> products are most commonly **offered by car dealerships**. They are colorless and exhibit a waxy texture that eventually solidifies. They require only one application and do not drip but will only be effective if applied liberally by a well-trained and conscientious technician.

    c. <u>Tar Based</u> approach is otherwise known as **undercoating**. It involves spraying a black, tar-like substance on the exposed parts of the underbody of your car, which then solidifies and acts as a permanent shield against moisture, salt, and other chemicals. The major risk to tar-based solutions is that if not applied properly and thoroughly, cracks may develop in the coating over time and trap moisture within itself, leading to rust. **Ziebart** is one of the largest providers of this method of rust protection and charges approximately $150 per vehicle.

2. **Electronic Module**. The favorite product for many business managers to sell is an Electronic Module which involves installing a small device in your car that then sends a weak electric current through the metal and in theory stops it from rusting. The Automobile Protection Association's website currently states "the APA is not convinced that electronic anti-rust devices provide good protection compared to the available alternatives. We do not recommend them." A recent check of the suppliers of these devices indicates that these modules no longer seem to be available at retailers. A number of investigative reports by news organizations in recent years has shown these modules to be of questionable value.

There is considerable debate regarding whether you should get rustproofing and lots of opinions as to which method is best. According to Consumer Reports, in their annual auto survey, "Today's vehicles are manufactured with good corrosion protection ... rust problems have almost vanished in modern vehicles." Ask about the car manufacturer's Rust Perforation Warranty. Most standard rust-through warranties for domestic and imported vehicles now run five years or more. **If you decide to get rustproofing on your vehicle (and decide to do it at the dealership), understand what it is costing and do not accept the first offer!**

Rip-Off #2 - "Police Traceable" Etching

Most car dealers (new and used) try to charge additional fees to increase the profit on the car. The fees will have names such as Doc Fees, Admin Fees, Security Package, Security Etching, Nitrogen, Road Hazard Protection, Key Fob Protection, and lots of others. Your first duty is to **make sure all charges are explained** and ask yourself if they make sense. Then, negotiate them off the deal or reduce the cost being quoted. If the dealer cannot **explain the benefit** provided by each and why it is worth what they are charging, have it removed or reduced. Some of the benefits are nice to have but the dealer's cost to provide these protections is very low compared to what is typically charged so there is usually room to negotiate the fees lower. You can be assured that dealers routinely overcharge for these extras.

Rip-Off #3 - Life & Other Insurance

Here is another area where the dealership can often take advantage of an unprepared car buyer and offer <u>a good product at an inflated price</u>. There is a great case to be made for protecting yourself against a situation where you cannot make the finance payments on your car. Those might include <u>losing your job</u>, short term or long term <u>disability</u>, catastrophic <u>illness</u>, or <u>death</u>. Once you have decided to purchase the vehicle, the Financial Services Manager (also called the Business Manager or Finance & Insurance Manager) will likely offer you the opportunity to protect yourself from Loss of Employment, Personal Injury or Disability, or Death by adding insurance policies that will provide the funds necessary to pay off the car loan and/or provide monthly income (in the case of employment loss or disability) to cover your car payments.

There are two issues here: <u>First</u>, you can usually *purchase the same coverage at your bank or insurance company that you already do business with at a fraction of the cost.* <u>Second</u>, the policies you buy at the dealership will be underwritten by *an insurer who may or may not be in business when and if you have to make a claim.* (In a worse case scenario, the dealership may be issuing the policy which would make it even riskier that you might not be able to collect). For example, if you are financing a $25,000 car purchase over 5 years, my recommendation would be to consider getting a five-year term life insurance policy for $25,000 from a reputable financial institution of your choice plus private disability insurance for the same period. It is likely that you can do it at less than half the cost of buying this at the dealership and with less risk. Your bank or car insurance company is the first place to go to get a quote and find out what you will need.

Rip-Off #4 - Demo Vehicles

Most new car dealerships have demonstrator vehicles that are used for test drives by prospective customers. These vehicles usually cover a cross section of the brand product line and are driven by the management and sales team. At a typical dealership, each team member uses the demo for personal use and makes sure the vehicle is available for test drives during business hours. These cars usually go on the road for up to 15,000 kilometers (about 10,000 miles) and, prior to that point, they are taken off the road and sold at a discount as demonstrator vehicles. These vehicles normally still qualify as "new cars" (if they are under 15,000 kilometers) so they may still be eligible for the new car incentives available from the factory. Because demos are normally discounted to clear them off the lot, you can save money by buying a demo, however, consider the following if you are contemplating a demo;

- You will lose some of the new car warranty that you would normally get (i.e., if the car has 10,000 km on it, you will lose that from the mileage allowance).

- The discount may not be enough to offset the mileage and wear and tear that you are agreeing to accept.

- Only if you are lucky, will you find that the demo that is available perfectly matches the trim level, package and color that you wanted.

Most often, a demo will be a compromise or you will be paying the same amount (as you would for the new car that you actually wanted) for a demo with a few more features that you really don't need or want and a driving history that is somewhat unknown.

In my experience, here is how most demos get sold: a customer comes to the dealership and decides on a specific model, trim level, and color. The salesperson or Sales Manager then approaches the customer with an alternative: ***"We have a demo that has some additional features that we could get you for the same price/payment. Would you like to consider it?"*** Now, if you really wanted the car with leather seats and the demo is the only way you can fit it into your budget, this might be your lucky day, however, be aware that this switch is being offered because it benefits the dealership.

Chapter 4

TEN MISTAKES TO AVOID WHEN VISITING A DEALERSHIP

Mistake #1 - Arriving Unprepared

I guess it's obvious you should arrive prepared but many people don't know how to be prepared for a visit to the showroom. Here's the basic stuff you must have done before arriving:

- Have a list of the vehicles that you have researched either online or from recommendations by family and friends. What I mean is Make, Model, Trim, and Package if possible. For example, Make = **Nissan**, Model = **Rogue**, Trim = **SV**, and Package = **Technology Package**. In this example, a Nissan Rogue (in Canada) sells for between $26,148 and $36,998 (MSRP) (depending on the Trim and Package - which, in the example used, is $33,433 + Freight, PDI, and taxes). That's a big difference in price and features. Make sure you know what ballpark you are playing in.

- Use the "build and price" tool available on the manufacturer's website (as well as on most dealership websites) to understand the Models, Trims, and Packages as well as what lease or finance payment is reasonable for the Make, Model, and Trim level you have on your list. For example, if you build the *2018 Nissan Rogue SV-AWD with Technology Package* on the Nissan Canada website, your **payments** (at full list price and not including taxes) would be:
    - **Lease Payments** with 20,000 Km/Year Allowance will be:
        - 24 Month Lease = $519 per month + tax
        - 36 Month Lease = $436 per month + tax
        - 48 Month Lease = $404 per month + tax
        - 60 Month Lease = $388 per month + tax
    - **Finance Payments** (where you own the vehicle) will be:
        - 24 Month Term = $1,452 per month + tax
        - 36 Month Term = $968 per month + tax
        - 48 Month Term = $726 per month + tax
        - 60 Month Term = $594 per month + tax
        - 72 Month Term = $513 per month + tax
        - 84 Month Term = $459 per month + tax
- Have a list of questions. Regardless of how much research you do in advance, you should have questions that you need answered in order to clarify some aspects of the vehicle, the financing, the warranties on the vehicle, or the availability of the model on your list.

Remember, there are no stupid questions, however, by asking questions that address your particular concerns, you will quickly discover whether the salesperson you meet at the dealership is someone you want to do business with. Incomplete answers or outright evasion of questions will be the sign that you should be shopping elsewhere. If you have arrived prepared but the salesperson is not ready to answer all your questions and concerns, it's a good predictor that the rest of the process is not going to go smoothly. Find someone you feel is qualified to provide the level of service you deserve.

Mistake #2 - Bypassing the Used Car Lot

When I bought my first car, it was a new car and I kicked myself for the next 5 years for making such a bad decision. In those days, the only way to finance a car was to go to the bank and get a car loan, and, the rates were not very "competitive" because there was really no competition for car loans. As a result, I was saddled with a short amortization period and car payments that ate up most of my disposable income. But, I had a shiny new car to drive!

In those days, I probably would have been better off to buy a used car, fix it up, and save myself interest costs and have money for other things. Today, however, the cars and the financing options are much different. On today's motor vehicles (even if they are 4 or 5 years old), the amount of electronics and computer equipment makes doing your own repairs and maintenance almost impossible. Cars now are safer and more reliable but if something goes wrong, they are a lot more expensive to fix. I remember tuning carburetors, checking the spark plug timing, and doing oil changes. Other than oil changes, you need a laptop computer and the manufacturer's software to do the other routine chores. And, by the way, carburetors are now only found in museums.

So, Are You Better to Buy a Pre-Owned Car or a New Car?

First time car buyers have a choice of buying a brand new car or buying a used car. Which is better? There are advantages and disadvantages to either choice. Most people would rather have a brand new car with its new- car smell and latest style, but there are reasons that a new car might not be the best choice. Let's take a look at the pros and cons of buying new and buying used.

Advantages of Buying New

- You get a brand new car with new-car feel and smell
- You get the latest styling, technology, and safety equipment
- You get a full manufacturer's warranty
- You get the option to lease (and buy or return at the end of the lease)
- You may get special manufacturer-sponsored pricing and low rate financing

Disadvantages of Buying New

- The value of a new car depreciates rapidly in the first year or two
- Insurance rates may be higher than for a used car

Advantages of Buying Used

- You save the high first-year depreciation of value
- If you buy almost-new, you may get the same styling and technology as a new car, at a lower price and still be able to access low finance rates provided via the manufacturer
- You get price flexibility by choosing between different model years, mileage, and condition
- You may buy "certified" vehicles with inspection and warranty – at a higher cost

Disadvantages of Buying Used

- You buy an "as-is" vehicle unless some manufacturer warranty remains on the vehicle
- You may be buying someone else's problem, unless you have your vehicle inspected
- You risk buying a wrecked or salvage vehicle, unless you run a CarProof or CarFax Vehicle History Report
- You typically don't have a lease option

- You may pay higher interest rates if you finance the car
- You may get fewer safety features that are otherwise available on current cars

Summary

To summarize, buying a used car can be a better value for your money but it comes with higher risks. Any used car purchase should include an extensive test drive, an inspection by a qualified mechanic, and a **CarFax or CarProof Vehicle History Report**. (CarProof is the Canadian standard and CarFax covers the US, although both are owned by the same company – IHS Markit). Also consider buying an extended warranty (preferably from the vehicle manufacturer).

Some brands provide *Certified Pre-Owned* programs through their franchise dealers where recent model year used vehicles that pass a rigorous inspection can qualify for additional warranty and manufacturer subsidized finance rates. These vehicles cost a bit more but provide the peace of mind that may be keeping you from considering a used car. These CPO programs are only available at franchise dealers and only from automotive brands that have a CPO program in place. The largest Used Car Superstores replicate this type of program as a way to complete with franchise dealers.

If you're considering an almost-new vehicle, make sure you can't get the same vehicle, new, at about the same price, which can happen if the manufacturer is offering special promotional deals (particularly at the end of the Model Year).

My Opinion on the Debate

Even though I regretted it on my first car, I believe that <u>conditions now favor buying new over used for most people most of the time</u>. The exception occurs if you are paying cash. You can save real dollars by buying a two-year-old car and having the original owner effectively paying for the depreciation. But if you finance the used car, it's very likely that the depreciation you saved on the purchase will be offset by the higher interest you will pay on a used car loan. New cars are coming with financing rates as low as 0% plus you may qualify for one or more special incentives provided by the manufacturer such as a Loyalty Rebate, or Grad Rebate, or First Time Buyer Rebate, or one of several other incentives. Most of these perks are not available on used cars.

For someone buying a first car, the availability of very low interest rates on terms as long as 84 and 96 months on new cars means you can spread your payments out so your monthly commitment is low but the option of repaying the loan earlier is still available. This way, you get to drive a new car with the newest technologies without handcuffing yourself with unmanageable car payments. The risk is that your needs change significantly over the next few years such that you need to trade in the new car well before you have paid off enough of the loan to avoid taking a loss on the trade-in.

Mistake #3 - Failing to Take an Extended Test Drive

When you are in the market for a new or used vehicle, there is only so much research you can do online. At some point, you need to take your short list of vehicles and see how they fit and feel. No matter how the car looks on paper, if it doesn't connect with you in terms of comfort, ride, handling, or aesthetics, you will likely end up regretting your decision later.

Here are some things you should keep in mind as you head out to test drive your potential new vehicles.

- **Schedule Enough Time**. Take an afternoon or several evenings to do your test-drives and book a time with your salesperson so she or he can have the correct vehicle ready when you arrive. Don't book 4 or 5 test-drives back to back or you may find yourself rushed and/or unable to remember one vehicle from the other.

- **Ask Questions**. A good salesperson should be able to answer your questions about anything you're unfamiliar with. She or he can help you learn how to operate special features such as the Bluetooth system and should be ready to demonstrate how these features work on the test drive.

- **Set Your Route**. Discuss your route with the salesperson before you leave the lot. Try to drive through a range of landscapes during the test drive so you get a sense of how the car handles in different circumstances such as busy city streets, open highways, hills, bumps and tight corners. Your salesperson should have such a route already mapped out.

- **Comfort Quotient**. What are headroom and legroom like? Do you bump your head when you get in? Can you adjust your seat and seat belt to your satisfaction? Do the interior proportions feel right? Can you easily read the instrument panel and reach all the controls? Do they feel like they are of high quality? And, remember to check out sightlines and blind spots. Some cars look great from the outside but driver ergonomics and visibility issues can make the day-to-day use of the vehicle enjoyable or dreadful. Only an actual test drive will make it possible to answer these questions fully.

- **Give it a Workout**. Try as many manoeuvres as you can to see how the car handles. Find a quiet street or empty parking lot to test quick stops, acceleration and turning radius. Is the vehicle responsive? Can you control it easily? Also, include a turning circle test on the test drive. If you can turn it 180 degrees on a side street in one movement, the car should be nimble enough for most situations you will encounter.

- **Listen**. Don't let the salesperson's pitch distract you from focusing on the drive: it's okay to ask for a quiet time to just listen to the car. In fact, during the test drive, the salesperson

38

should only be speaking when you have questions to ask. (That's why I prefer to be on the test drive with customers because questions or concerns can be dealt with at the time when they come up). Turn off the radio too, so you can listen for any unusual engine or road noises.

- **Drive it Twice.** Don't hesitate to go away and think about your experience before returning to the dealership for another test drive. It's better to be sure than to live with nagging doubts. At the same time, once you take the car on a complete test drive, you should know pretty quickly whether there is a "connection" with the vehicle. Some customers agonize over which car to choose (even when they have found the perfect car) because they're convinced there might be another vehicle out there that is even "more perfect". I believe you will discover that, when you find it, you'll know it. Because there is no shortage of quality vehicles on the market today, your goal of test-driving a few short-listed vehicles is to determine (in a reasonably rational process) whether one car really "speaks to you". If you make a "connection" with a car that passes the above tests, it's a good sign that you have found that special vehicle that you will enjoy owning for years to come.

Mistake #4 - Not Booking an Appointment

I recently booked an appointment with my doctor. I gave him an indication of the reason for the visit when I booked the appointment so he was prepared for our meeting. The time we spent together was not long but the assistance and advice I received was extremely helpful and actionable. During our meeting, I had the doctor's undivided attention. I only wish that a larger portion of the people coming to the dealership would take this approach. It works in most other situations where you are making a major purchase or decision and are seeking expertise and assistance.

Many of the people who have bought cars from me booked an appointment (if not to buy the car) to get advice on what vehicle or lease/financing option would best suit their needs. For those dealerships located in a high traffic auto-mall, the people coming to the store often just arrive at random. I am always puzzled by people who wander from dealership to dealership when they are in the market for a car. It does not seem to be the most productive use of one's time (unless, of course, you have read this guide in which case you will be well prepared to handle any situation that you encounter).

If you want to talk to the most experienced and knowledgeable people at the dealership, your chances of meeting one by just wandering in are somewhat limited. Chances are higher that you will be "picked up" by one of the junior salespeople on the floor whose product knowledge is sketchy and whose assessment skills are in the development stage (despite how enthusiastic they might be). Meanwhile, the most experienced and knowledgeable salespeople are busy meeting with prospects who have booked appointments.

Most people in the market for a car do some research online and talk to friends or family about what brands or models should be considered. You probably have two or three cars on your short list. This is the point where I always recommend that you contact a dealership or a specific car salesperson recommended by someone you trust or contact your local dealership to find an experienced professional to assist you. You can call the Sales Manager and ask that you be put in touch with the dealership's best sales consultant or simply go to the dealership website and complete one of the forms for information on the model of interest.

When you inquire online, you will normally be dealing with one of the senior salespeople at the dealership (as most car dealerships have online requests handled by the Internet Manager). Now, you can get some basic questions answered before you book an appointment. When you arrive at the dealership, you have someone specific to meet and the sales consultant can have the specific models of interest lined up for you to consider. The other advantage of handling your car buying process in this way is that you are dealing with a member of the dealership management who is equipped to find all the manufacturer incentives for which you qualify as well as having the authority to work out a special deal for you that might not otherwise be available to someone just walking in off the street.

If you want to be treated like a V.I.P., it's best to book an appointment just like you would if you were planning to buy a house, setting up a program with a fitness trainer, or taking a golf lesson. Or, you can wander into a dealership at random and hope you get lucky.

Mistake #5 - Not Researching the Value of Your Trade-in Vehicle

Among the early lessons my father taught me about economics was that **things are worth what someone is willing to pay for them**. When it's time to trade or sell a pre-owned vehicle, car owners obviously want the maximum value for it. At the very least, they want fair market value. Sometimes it's difficult to separate the emotional value (i.e., only you know what a wonderful car it's been for the past 10 years and 250,000 Km) from the economic value.

But "fair market value" (or economic value) often differs from the perceived value that a customer has in mind. In fact, customers are frequently disappointed to learn their vehicles are worth less than they anticipated — sometimes several thousand dollars less.

Many factors go into determining what a dealership (or a private buyer) will pay for a vehicle, including the original MSRP

41

(Manufacturer's Suggested Retail Price), mechanical condition, physical appearance, mileage, market conditions, accessories, brand, model type, maintenance history, accident history, etc.

To avoid a shock when you get to the dealership and have your trade-in appraised, I suggest customers take 5 minutes to check out the trade-in value of their vehicle on **CanadianBlackBook.com** (use Kelley Blue Book in the US at **KBB.com**). You can plug in the Year, Make, Model, mileage, and equipment on your vehicle and quickly get a range of what is being paid (in your geographic area) for comparable vehicles (by dealers). I get a lot of customers who check prices on **autoTRADER** (which provides a listing of what private sellers and dealers are **asking** for used vehicles). Remember, these are retail prices for certified and re-conditioned (if bought at a dealership) vehicles, whereas your trade- in is an **As-Is**, uncertified vehicle being sold wholesale. Your trade-in vehicle can be worth what is being asked on Autotrader once it is reconditioned, detailed, certified and includes a vehicle history report.

If you arrive at the dealership with a reasonable idea of the wholesale and retail values for your trade-in vehicle, you are better able to negotiate a fair price. If your vehicle is accident-free and in good condition, you are in a position to hold out for a price at the higher end of the value range. If the used car manager feels your trade-in can be put on the lot without major reconditioning costs, he will often be persuaded to pay a little above "fair market value" for your trade-in if it is the key to closing the deal on the new vehicle.

Mistake #6 - Landing on the Wrong Car (for your needs)

Whenever you sit down with a sales consultant at a car dealership, you can expect to be asked a lot of questions. By the way, if it feels like an interrogation, you're not sitting with a true professional. *A good* *salesperson will want to have a <u>conversation</u> where he/she learns about your situation, what kind of cars you have owned until now, and get an idea of the kind of vehicle that might fit your needs and desires at this point in your life.* The better the salesperson understands your situation, the better he/she can help you select the car that is perfect for you. It might even be a model or trim package that you had not considered but is a great fit.

Now, if your reaction is to be a bit suspicious about car salespeople anyway, you might find answering a lot of questions to be uncomfortable and somewhat intrusive. Rather than being offended, you should consider this as a mark of a trained sales professional who is interested in you as well as in matching you up with a vehicle that fits your lifestyle and budget. Despite the fact that you may have checked out the various Trim levels and Packages online, a good salesperson will be able to make suggestions (either product or financing related) that may not have been evident in your online research.

When I have met with customers for the first time (whether in person at the dealership or online), I am most interested in understanding: **What transportation problem are you trying to solve?** To understand this, I need to know what you are driving now (maybe you're taking the bus), what vehicles are already in the household, what's been happening with your shopping experience so far, and what information you already have (as well as what information you still need to feel comfortable about making a decision).

These are questions you should be asking yourself as well. <u>Why is your car falling a bit short of what you need</u>? It's also helpful to know <u>if anything in your life has changed recently</u> (or is about to change) where you need something different or better. And, since you have arrived at the showroom, <u>what is it about this Brand, Model, or Dealership that you believe might make it the best choice</u>? With this information, which only takes a few minutes to acquire, I am in a

43

pretty good position to pick out a couple of possible products that will fit the bill. The alternative is to guess and spend time considering and test driving several models only to discover we are on the wrong car. Since that's not very productive for you nor the salesperson, it's much better to take a little time up front and clarify the transportation problem you came to the dealership to solve.

Mistake #7 - Letting the Emotion of the Situation Overtake Your Judgment

It is easy to take this caution lightly and think, "Don't worry, I am quite capable of handling my emotions, thank you!". However, the modern car dealership and the people who work there have developed a process that is pretty effective in moving most people from calm and cool to excited and ready to agree to things they might otherwise vigorously scrutinize. *Every step of the process has been planned and choreographed in advance* to move you from a mildly interested shopper to an enthusiastic buyer. It's OK to enjoy the "ride" as long as you do not lose sight of the fact that the whole process is rigged to get you to buy a car today. If you are open to that possibility (because you have prepared for your visit), then have some fun but keep one hand on your wallet. At the end of the process, you want to make an informed and rational decision but you can do that and still enjoy the process.

Mistake #8 - Blowing Your Budget (or Not Having a Budget)

As is the case with any major purchase, it is not uncommon to end up spending more than you expected by the time the process is completed. In fact, **I would be surprised if you went car shopping with a rough idea of what you expected to pay and actually came in under your "budget"**. It almost never happens that way. The truth is, everything costs more than what we expect and what we want to pay for it. Nevertheless, it is your responsibility to sketch out, in advance, the monthly outflows that a new car will involve and decide where your "comfort zone" ends. Here's the list of cash costs to tally:

- Finance/Lease payments (including all taxes and fees)
- Insurance Coverage. Talk to your insurance company or broker in advance and ask about the cars on your short list and what coverage will be needed as well as the cost. (Some cars are more expensive to insure than others)
- Gas & Maintenance. If this is your first car, you may be trading bus fare for gas station charges. If you are moving from an old car to a new car, you should find that the improved mileage will save you on gas. Maintenance expenses on a new car should be near zero for the first few years (as the manufacturer's standard warranties will cover anything serious) but maintenance on used cars starts to accelerate once they get past 4 years old.
- Savings. Also consider that there should be gas savings, possibly insurance savings, and maintenance savings that will result from moving from an old clunker to a new (or newer) car. Those should also be factored into your monthly budget.

Sometimes car buyers get stuck on a monthly number that they have set and are reluctant to exceed it by even a dollar. Usually you will find that the car you really want will put you over your budget. That's why you should have a budget but <u>also consider what you could live with if you found the absolutely perfect vehicle</u>. If you allow for this possibility in your planning, you have a better chance of getting exactly the car you want without blowing the budget (maybe just stretching it a bit).

Mistake #9 - Saying You are "Not Buying Today"

Based on my experience in the car business and the evolution I have been seeing recently in manufacturers and dealers becoming more focused on delighting and retaining customers, I offer the following suggestions that I guarantee will get you a great deal without wasting time:

- <u>Arrive at the dealership as a buyer</u>. Too often, car buyers get off on the wrong foot by coming to a dealership and indicating very early that they have no plans to buy today. This is understandable; you don't want to be rushed into a decision and you want to communicate to the salesperson that you will be "on guard" for any pressure tactics. However, the experienced car sales professional is not put off by your "not buying today" declaration. In fact, the real pros will consider it a challenge to overcome. What you want to avoid is a confrontational encounter, so your best strategy when buying a car is to *identify yourself as a buyer, not a shopper*. Don't be defensive; simply present yourself as an easy buyer to deal with. The customer who approaches a car dealer in a defensive and pushy manner, tends to cause the dealership personnel to respond the same way. If you want to play games, there is no shortage of salespeople capable of operating in that realm. Make it clear you are ready to buy as long as you find the right vehicle and the deal offered is fair. Now watch how well you get treated.

- <u>Price should not be your greatest concern</u>. Let the salesperson know that price is not your biggest concern but that the car is your main focus. This will be well received by the salesperson and encourage them to provide the full level of service you deserve. Let them know that you know that agreeing on price is easy once the car is right. This is going to make the sales process quicker by reducing confrontation and later, will make getting your best possible terms even easier (because you have already confirmed you plan to buy <u>if</u> the offer is a fair one).

- <u>Determine the right car for you</u>. Contrary to strategies of the past, the best way to determine the right vehicle is not online or on the phone but at the dealership. A trick to make sure you are on the right vehicle is to look at the vehicles just above and just below what you think you want. Any interest you have in either of the other two product choices means you are not yet on the perfect product for you. Before you go further, make sure you have identified the car that is exactly what you need and want.

- <u>Test-drive the vehicle</u>. Driving the vehicle will actually save you time negotiating and makes the dealership feel like they have done their job and provides them with more confidence in giving you their best price. Besides, until you drive the vehicle, you cannot know if it feels like the vehicle you want to be spending a lot of time with for the next 5 or 10 years. Dealerships also understand that you cannot make a firm commitment to purchase unless you have driven the vehicle and (by doing so) understand the full value of the offer in front of you.

- <u>Request a fully documented proposal</u>. Ask the dealership to present their offer to you including price, trade figures, purchase and lease payments, down payments and interest rates as well as rebates and incentives that you are qualified to receive, all at one time.

- <u>Determining a fair price</u>? Franchised car dealers in Canada and the US operate on about the same net margins as a grocery store (i.e., 2% net margin - after all expenses). Most transactions generate more money to government taxes than profits to the dealer. Based on this reality, use your own logic to make sense of what is a fair price to offer the dealer. Your dealer will love this logic and remove time and pain from the process. It is outdated thinking to believe that you have to shop 5 or 6 locations to get a good deal. The next time you are ready to get something new just follow my steps; let your dealer know you are there to buy, be sure you are on the right car, ask that they present their proposal in writing, and lastly, enter the discussion of value and pricing issues with a positive and respectful attitude and I guarantee you a great deal!

Mistake #10 - Starting with "Just Give Me Your Best Price"

On a fairly regular basis, some of our less sophisticated shoppers come to the dealership asking for our **"best price"**. <u>By simply asking this question in a dealership, there is no guarantee that you will get the dealership's "best price" (whatever that means to you).</u> Perhaps these people believe there is a secret no-go-below price on each vehicle that has been pre-determined by the owner and by just boldly asking for it, they will get it. On the contrary, I can guarantee you that no such list exists.

The truth is that we have the **Manufacturer's Suggested Retail Price (MSRP)** and we have the **dealer cost** (which is what the dealership paid the manufacturer for the car). **Somewhere between these two numbers is a number that the dealership will agree to accept,** however, this number will vary depending on a number of factors (some of which change by day and by week). For example, let's say the dealership has a new car in a color that has been unpopular and the Sales Manager just got a lecture from the Dealer Principal earlier that day that inventory turnover is below standard (based on the aged inventory report just run). If someone comes into the store interested in that particular vehicle today (in the hard-to-sell color), he might agree to move that vehicle at any firm offer above dealer cost to get the inventory moving in the right direction. On the same car in a more popular color, he might not be so flexible.

Of course, the dealership's "best price" is the MSRP (where they make a fair but not excessive profit) and the dealership's "worst price" is the dealer cost where they make nothing on the car. Sometimes dealerships will sell a car at their "worst price" for a variety of reasons including the one mentioned above. For example, **it's the end of the month and the Sales Manager needs a few more deals to hit a target for the month** (maybe that target represents a sales bonus). Or, it is the last day of a major sales event on which the Dealer Principal has spent a considerable amount on advertising and promotion. It's easier for the Sales Manager to explain that a few of the deals were "skinny" than to explain why the target was missed (by a few units). That's how the business works in the real world.

The concept of "Supply and Demand" also plays into determining the "best price". Cars that are in short supply are seldom discounted while those that the dealer knows are backed up on lots across the district are more likely to be discounted (beyond the incentives provided by the manufacturer). It is difficult for the average car shopper to know (by brand and by dealership) what dynamics are at work on a particular day or week. By the same token, it is difficult for the salesperson (or even the Sales Manager) to know what crazy deal he/she might ultimately agree to do until faced with a serious buyer on a particular car that he/she has been trying to sell for months.

If you are a car buyer and you find yourself in such a situation where you are on a car that the Sales Manager feels "must" be sold and you have negotiated a great deal, you should take advantage of the leverage you have and do the deal. I have seen customers walk away from outstanding opportunities where they had the Sales Manager over-a-barrel because they wanted to "think about it" only to return a day or two later to find the deal had been taken off the table (when the Sales Manager had returned to his/her senses). By the way, in most jurisdictions, it's only a "deal" when both parties have signed a purchase agreement.

And one last point: **the salesperson's job is <u>not</u> to negotiate a discounted price**. His/her job is to understand your vehicle needs and get you on a vehicle well suited to those needs (as well as to select a car that is affordable for you). The latter is a bit imprecise so if there is a disconnect between the regular price of the car and the price that the customer is willing to pay, the Sales Manager has the final authority. That's why <u>the salesperson will ask you for a formal signed offer</u> if you believe the price presented is unacceptable. If you caught the Sales Manager on the right day and right vehicle, you might find your offer accepted.

Chapter 5

HOW TO GET MAXIMUM DOLLARS FOR YOUR TRADE-IN

Do you think it is worth an hour of your time to get an extra $1,000 or more for your trade-in vehicle? It's a rhetorical question but my experience is that the vast majority of car buyers will complain that they are not getting a fair deal from the dealer for their trade-in yet often do little work to enhance the value of their trade. Don't leave money on the table. Here are some simple and straightforward actions you can take to determine what to reasonably expect for your vehicle on a trade-in and how you can maximize the amount the dealer will pay you.

<u>Clean it and take pictures</u>. At the very minimum, wash the exterior, vacuum and wipe down the interior, and take photos of your vehicle. For $100 - $150, you can get a local car detailer to do all this for you including an engine shampoo and deodorizer (especially important if you are a smoker) so your car looks its best and smells great. Then, look up your car's Year, Make, and Model on **autoTRADER** or **Cars.com** and notice the photos that appear on the listings. Note the typical shots that each listing shows. Take the same shots of your

trade-in vehicle. About a dozen will be plenty (half interior and half exterior shots). Use your smartphone. It's easy and your smartphone takes excellent high definition photos.

Marketing Your Trade. Whether you are trying to sell your trade to a dealer or to a private buyer, they are both looking for the same things:

- What are the special features of the vehicle? Is it accident-free? One owner? Special equipment such as leather interior, heated seats, Bluetooth phone system, premium sound system, navigation/GPS system, DVD entertainment system, sunroof, alloy wheels, extended (transferable) warranty protection? Do you have all the service records for the vehicle? Did you have the vehicle rust proofed? Document these features in a short written description. With 12+ photos of your car plus the disclosures just mentioned, you can approach a few dealers online and get a pretty good idea of what they are willing to offer (if you are trading in your vehicle on a specific new car).

- Go to the manufacturer's website for your vehicle (use Google to find the site) and look for specifications for the Year, Make, and Model of the vehicle you are trading. Usually you will find this information under the "Owners" tab where manuals, brochures, and spec sheets for prior model year vehicles can be found and downloaded. Find your Model and Year vehicle. You might discover facts about your car that you did not know. Determine your vehicle's trim level as there may be a significant difference between the entry-level trim and the luxury version of your car.

- Get the vehicle's service records. If you have not been keeping your service records in a file folder, go to any franchise dealer of your brand (if it's a Ford, go to a Ford dealership) and ask them to pull the service records directly from the factory. If the vehicle was serviced at a dealership, the manufacturer will have a record of all the work done. This information is normally also available by running a **CarFax or CarProof** report on your vehicle.

<u>How to determine a fair price</u>. Use **Black Book**, **Kelly Blue Book**, etc to get an idea of the trade-in prices being paid recently for your vehicle. See how many exact matches you get when you search for your exact Year, Make, Model, and Trim level on sites such as **autoTRADER, Cars.com, CarGurus, Kijiji**, etc. Look for how many cars are in a 500 km (300 mile) radius and also check competitors. For example, if you are trading a four year old Honda Civic (a 4-door compact sedan), check how many Toyota Corolla, Mazda3, Hyundai Elantra, and Chevy Cruze vehicles are also up for sale. This will give you a quick picture of the state of the market. Remember that cars being offered by dealers and private sellers are listed at <u>retail selling prices</u> on <u>safety certified and often reconditioned units</u> (not the wholesale buying prices being paid by the dealer for an "as-is" vehicle).

Keep in mind that the dealer will either buy your trade for the purpose of reselling it on their used car lot or to sell it to a wholesaler. Either way, the dealer needs to find a buyer for your "as-is" vehicle if the plan is to put your vehicle on the used car lot, the price the dealer is willing to pay will be based on how much it will cost to do any reconditioning work and to safety certify the vehicle plus a reasonable profit while being able to sell your vehicle at a competitive price. <u>The dealer is going to take 100% of the risk of re-selling your "as-is" vehicle which is typically 45 to 60 days</u>. During this period, the dealer will incur expenses such as advertising, clean up costs, and interest expenses to finance his used car inventory. Most dealers now use sophisticated software to guide them in determining a reasonable market price/value and prepare an exit strategy (i.e., what price and timeframe will be required to sell your vehicle) based on the current used car market for your type of vehicle. If there is an over-supply of your specific vehicle, the dealer will need to be extra aggressive in pricing and marketing your vehicle in order to move it in a reasonable time. Alternatively, if supply of your specific type of vehicle is heavy and demand is weak, the dealer will be reluctant to pay what **Black**

Book or other reference sources suggest is the market value for your vehicle. Some portions of the used car market can change quickly.

<u>Test the market</u>. With the research you have done online and the photos you have taken, you can contact dealers directly and post your vehicle on **autoTRADER** or a similar site to see what level of interest there is out there. I recommend you use these tools only as research to understand where there is a market for your vehicle. Selling a vehicle privately has some danger associated with it not to mention the inconvenience of inviting strangers to your home and taking them out on test drives. Once you have received feedback from your small marketing program, use the information collected to approach a large used car dealer or a new car franchise dealer from a position of knowledge.

If you do the merchandising work I have recommended above, you will be justified in asking for a quote on your vehicle without even visiting the dealership. Ask for a quote on the exact new car you have selected along with a firm quote on your trade-in vehicle and you should be able to secure a firm quote. Then you need only to visit the dealer to confirm the price on your trade-in and test drive the new car.

Chapter 6

HOW TO WIN THE BATTLE WITH THE BUSINESS OFFICE

So you have moved through the purchase process and agreed to buy or lease a vehicle at terms and conditions that you can live with (even though you pushed the limit of the budget you had set in advance). You're pretty happy to have worked out what you feel is a good (maybe even, a great) deal. You're looking forward to actually driving your new purchase as soon as licensing and detailing can be completed. But before that can happen, you need to take care of some paperwork.

You are about to meet the **Business Manager** (also called the Finance Manager, the F&I Manager, the Financial Services Manager, Loan Officer even the Delivery Coordinator) but they are all the same person. Whoever holds this position is one of the top salespeople in the dealership because they have demonstrated their ability to quickly and efficiently separate customers (that's you who has just bought a car) from their money. I know, you already signed the purchase agreement that outlines pretty clearly what you agreed to pay for the car but it was probably the result of some tough negotiating to achieve a nice discount on the vehicle. Well, the Business Manager's job is to recover that money that the dealership failed to get on the transaction and then pad it as much as possible.

Before you formally meet this person, you will be led to believe that this is the most friendly and helpful person at the dealership. The Business Manager is highly qualified in all matters relating to getting your financing and licensing set up properly and will take you through the paperwork, your delivery, and further help you by putting together your finance/lease application with the bank. The person you meet will almost always be charming and possess a pleasant and cordial (even friendly) demeanour. But, you must remember two important facts:

1. You are NOT OBLIGATED to purchase any of the products or services he/she offers including extra fees and administrative charges.

2. However, the Business Manager IS OBLIGATED by the Dealer Principal to sell you products to help increase profits for the dealership. The rule in the Business Office is to do whatever it takes to sell you rustproofing, extra warranty protection, and other "protection packages" even if mis-representation and the occasional outright lie is necessary to get it done. They'll start with friendly chat and filling out forms to get you comfortable and then gradually transition into the "fear" campaign that is hard to resist. Because, when it becomes a question of protecting your family and your vehicle "investment", you will find it hard to say "no" to the very persuasive Business Manager.

Let's be clear. The automotive retail industry is not really much different than other big-ticket retail establishments. The main purchase item is not where the profit is made. For example, the electronics retailer does not make much on the large flat screen TV. Most of the profit on the transaction comes from selling HDMI cables, mounting hardware and warranties. It's also true with clothing. The business suit you buy at a clothing retailer is the big ticket item that's on sale at 50% off and gets you in the store but the profit is made on selling you a couple of shirts, ties, a belt, and maybe a new pair of shoes. Car dealerships are much the same.

Car dealerships are finding it increasingly difficult to make much, if any, profit on the actual sale of a new car. There is just too much information readily available to car shoppers about true discounts on new cars. When I got into the car business over a decade ago, it was possible to average $1,000+ profit on a mid-sized sedan. Now, it is less than half that figure. Therefore there is even greater pressure to make the money on the "backend" where the Business Manager is the last line of defence in the dealer's quest to secure a "reasonable" profit on the vehicle.

The Business Manager's key message will be that having now acquired this expensive new asset, you will want to protect your investment. Everything being pitched will have this underlying message, i.e., the products and services being offered are meant to benefit you and your family. It's hard to argue that you wouldn't want to protect your new vehicle. And, to be fair, some of the insurance-related products are meant to protect you from unforeseen calamities such as job loss, theft, and road hazards. These will be part of the <u>fear campaign</u>.

Here's what you will most likely be offered when you meet the Business Manager:

1. **Rustproofing**. Before you get the pitch on rustproofing, you should know that every new car from any manufacturer has more that adequate corrosion protection. In fact, third party application of rust proofing chemicals can potentially void your new car warranty. (Manufacturers tend to ignore this when their franchise dealer does the rustproofing, however, a poorly done rustproofing job can plug drain channels in car body panels resulting in moisture collecting and eventually doing the damage the rustproofing was meant to prevent). The reason dealers lead off their pitch with rustproofing is because the

profit margins are so high. I have seen rustproofing packages sell for from $500 to $2,500 when the premium sound deadening packages are sold. (And the cost to apply these chemicals is less than a couple of hundred dollars). If you think you still want rustproofing on your new car, check pricing at Krown & other outside sources. If the price offered by the dealer is the same (which it will not be without considerable negotiation), then the dealer applied product has the advantage that it can be rolled into your monthly payment (instead of a cash outlay after you leave the dealership). Here are two rustptoofing solutions normally offered:

a. Chemicals. The dealer will offer a lifetime warranty on the spray-in rustproofing but consider that new vehicles are built with galvanized steel and covered with multiple layers of paint and clear coat coverings so the vehicle's body should last for 10 years whether you rustproof it or not. If you live in a northern climate where snow and ice mean salt and other chemicals are used liberally to keep roads passable, you will want to keep salt off your vehicle during the winter by running it through a car wash every month. But even if your rustproofed vehicle develops rust after six or seven years, the dealership's warranty will only cover the cost up to the value of the car. It is very seldom (if ever) that the dealer will payout on a rustproofing warranty. Even the 7 to 10 year rust perforation warranty offered by most manufacturers now is a pretty safe offer.

b. Electronic Rust Module. It has become popular with Business Managers at dealerships to recommend a quickly-installed device called a rust module. It's a small box that applies a weak electric current to the metal on your vehicle based on the concept of reversing the flow of electrons out of the metal in the chemical reaction between steel, air, and water (which generates rust). This cathodic protection used on the submerged parts of bridges and boat motors is the story you will get from the Business Manager. It's all baloney with no facts or studies to prove it works on cars (that are normally not spending time under water). You will be told it is transferable from one vehicle to the next. You can buy these and install them yourself for $100 (if you believe the hype). The dealership will charge you many times that amount.

2. **Fabric Protection**. The next item is highly profitable and can sell for $100 to $200 or more. The truth is, you can do this one yourself by getting a spray can of <u>ScotchGard</u> at your local retailer and spray all the fabric surfaces. That's exactly what the dealer does and charges many times his cost for the service. It turns out that car manufacturers install high quality fabrics with stain and spill resistant treatments already built into the material. The Business Manager will tell you that the dealership Fabric Protection comes with a lifetime guarantee which means if you come back with a complaint, they will respray your upholstery. You would be wise to pass on this package and get the $10 can of <u>ScotchGard</u> at your local retailer.

3. **Paint Protection**. The sales pitch on this protection package often talks about the pollutants in the atmosphere combined with UV (ultraviolet) rays and their negative effect on your car's paint. However, modern car paints come with multiple clear coat layers and will benefit more from regular washing with a mild soap and water than from chemical "sealers" that are part of the paint protection pitch. Pass on this one as well and get a bottle of <u>Simoniz</u> car wax and a buffing cloth at the local automotive parts retailer and save hundreds.

4. **Etching** (for Theft Protection). This product has been around for a long time and the term "etching" refers to the "old days" when the lot attendant would use a small stencil and some mercuric acid to etch code numbers on each of the glass windows on the vehicle. The code numbers would be registered with the insurance company used by the dealership so if the vehicle was stolen, the "police traceable" etching numbers would help identify it. If the car was never recovered, your participation in the program (at a cost of anywhere from $399 to $999) would pay you $3,000 to $5,000 toward the purchase of a replacement vehicle. Any of the programs I have seen all expired after one to three years so it works out to be expensive insurance. Now most etching programs no longer bother with the messy business of etching glass surfaces. Most cars on dealer lots now have a half dozen stickers with registered code numbers applied to various vehicle body parts. They can be applied in about 2 minutes and that's how it works. Most dealers claim that they have to charge you for the etching since it's already part of the vehicle but just pass on this gimmick and watch that it doesn't find its way onto the purchase agreement when you're not looking.

5. **Gap Protection** (Insurance). This is very important and an often misunderstood product so please read this carefully. If you are financing or leasing your vehicle, **you should get GAP Insurance**. Here's why. If you financed all or most of your vehicle (i.e., little or no down payment), the value of your car almost as soon as you drive it off the lot, will be lower than the amount you borrowed to pay for it. This difference is the GAP between what your car is worth and what you owe on your loan. In fact, you will have a gap for the first couple of years of ownership. So, if you are involved in an accident (and your car is a total loss - written off), your insurance company will pay you the value of your car at the time of the crash. But that will not cover the "gap" that you need to clear the loan. Gap

Insurance means you do not have to worry about this situation. Your loan will be paid off and you can start fresh on a replacement vehicle. What the Finance Manager will not tell you is that <u>you can probably buy Gap Insurance from your own car insurance company</u> for less than $100 while the dealership will charge you 5 or 10 times that amount when they roll it into your monthly payment. Talk to your insurance company before heading for the dealership and ask about *GAP* insurance as well as *Loss of Employment* insurance (which the Business Manager will likely be pitching as well). LoE insurance is also a good idea but, again, your insurance company probably can cover you for less than what the dealer will offer.

6. **Extended Warranties**. Even though I do not normally buy extended warranty protection on household electronics (such as cell phones and flat screen TVs), I always recommended to my car buying customers to <u>match extended warranty protection with the term of their car loan</u>. If the standard factory warranty expires after 36 months (which most do) but you have a 72 month loan, you are going to be in a financial pinch if you end up with a major component failure at, say, the 65 month point. Covering yourself until the car is paid off can be a good thing. <u>That's the reason to do it</u> even if the Business Manager tells you that the bank wants you to have this coverage or "this is what most people go with". It's true that some warranties are not worth the paper they are written on (especially third party warranties). Normally <u>warranties purchased from the manufacturer are best</u> (they will be around if you need to make a claim), while warranties bought through the dealership are not even as good as the dealership's reputation. You could be buying a third party warranty and be led to believe it is a manufacturer's warranty. Be sure it is a warranty written by the manufacturer.

7. **Document Fees and Delivery Fees**. "Doc Fees" are common across the US but less common in Canada (although frequently disguised by using other terms). The dealer's rationale is that they cover the costs associated with preparing the documents for your bank loan, licensing, and related costs. Don't pay more than $75 in "doc" fees. Most states allow dealers to charge "doc fees" and some states limit what can be charged, however many jurisdictions have no limits. Also, <u>do not pay delivery fees on a used car</u>. On a new car, any delivery fees were likely included in the factory charges paid by the dealer so they will be part of the dealer's cost. See Chapter 8 where this topic is covered under "What Fees Must I Pay on a New Car?"

8. **Business Office Smoke & Mirrors.** A skilled Business Manager will often change the structure of the deal that you negotiated with the salesperson or the Sales Manager. He/she might change the price of the car and/or your trade to make room for products being offered. You might find your payment changed from monthly to biweekly or the term changed from 72 months to 84 months which can give the Business Manager an extra couple thousand dollars to work with <u>without changing your payment</u>. The key elements that can be modified (unless you are watching carefully) are: *Interest Rate*, *Down Payment*, *Monthly Payment*, and *Term of the Loan*. Here are a few tricks to watch for:

   a. <u>"Take your car home while we finish the paperwork"</u>. Never drive a car off the lot unless you have a properly signed and executed *purchase agreement and a loan agreement*. Dealerships often do this to "take you out of the market" while they try to get you approved or find a bank that will provide the maximum kickbacks. You end up getting a call a week later that the dealer had to change banks to get the loan approved and the payment will be $400 monthly instead of the $300 you agreed to pay. If your credit is not top notch, you are more susceptible to this scam.

b. <u>Switching the term of the loan from 72 months to 84 months</u>. Let's assume you went into the Business Office with a deal to finance your new car over 72 months at $350 per month, that's 72 x $350 = $25,200. If the Business Manager <u>switches it</u> to 84 months at the same payment, you are now paying 84 x $350 = $29,400. Presto, the Business Manager has just picked up $4,200. It is likely you will be offered some packages such as rust proofing, paint protection, loss of employment protection, etc. and eventually all these valuable goodies will be available for just $10 more on your payment (which then becomes $360 x 84 months = $30,240). Now you're out $5,040 since you walked into the office. Beware of the switch!

c. <u>Switching the payment frequency (Monthly to Biweekly)</u>. Many people get paid biweekly (every two weeks). Employers find this convenient because there are exactly 26 pay periods in a year (2 weeks x 26 = 52 weeks in a year). But since there are <u>roughly</u> four weeks in a month, people will almost always do some quick mental arithmetic to translate **a monthly payment into roughly two biweekly payments**. Of course, <u>this is not true</u>! For example, $150 biweekly (every two weeks) seems like it should be <u>about</u> $300 monthly. It is actually $325 monthly. It is a standard practice at many dealerships to give you a monthly payment going into the Business Office and have the Business Manager switch it to a biweekly payment to allow the addition of other packages while giving the illusion that the cost to you is a very small extra amount.

9. **<u>Menu Selling</u>**. A technique that is common in the Business Office is to group multiple products and/or services into packages to give the appearance of great value and to get away from trying to sell you each individual product on its own merits. This is called Menu Selling. There are usually three or four packages starting with Platinum that includes everything mentioned above as well as a few others, then a slightly scaled down Gold package, a Silver package, and a bare-bones Bronze package (which is often just Rust Proofing and Undercoat). Using this approach speeds up the sales process and makes it easier for the Business Manager to sell you at least the Bronze or Silver package. Try to construct your own "package" to eliminate the components of little or no value.

SUMMARY: I do not want to be overly harsh on the honest Business Managers who are trying to operate ethically, however, in most dealerships, the pressure is so great on the Business Managers to deliver big numbers in the "backend" that even the "straight arrows" I have met have been forced to employ varying degrees of deceptive practices to hold on to their jobs. I would like to give credit to the few dealers that are actually working at implementing fair and honest business practices, however they are a rare breed.

Chapter 7

THE DECISION TO LEASE OR BUY

According to JD Power (2018), most people finance their New Car (55%) or Used Car (54%) but on Used Cars, 43% pay cash while only 28% of New Car buyers pay cash. The balance of New Car buyers (28%) lease the vehicle. (Leasing is not normally available on Used Cars).

There are three ways to pay for a new car. *You can finance the vehicle, lease it, or just pay cash.* Leasing of cars has grown in popularity since the 2008 recession and seems to be accelerating in recent years. For a segment of the car buying public, leasing has always made a lot of sense and now, more of the general public is coming back to this form of financing.

Despite what some will tell you, leasing is simply a finance option that closely matches your typical buying cycle, allowing you to continually be driving a relatively new vehicle. The other big benefit that people have started to realize in recent years is that leasing eliminates the risk of negative equity! When you come to the end of your 36-month or 48-month lease, you either jump into a new lease or walk away (with no further obligation) or buy out the vehicle at a predetermined price. If you were 3 or 4 years into a 72 month or 84 month financing, you would likely be in a negative equity situation which means your car would be worth less than what you still owe the bank on your car loan. By financing, you are assuming all of the marketplace risk. You cannot know how much your vehicle will be worth in four or five years when you may want to trade it for something newer. With a lease, you know in advance exactly where you will stand at the end of the lease. And now, lease terms are as short as 12 to 24 months. This gives you additional options because until recently, only 36 month to 60 month leases were available from most manufacturers.

Leasing can provide some flexibility as well because a shorter term commitment is possible. Since *leasing means you are really only paying for the portion of the car you are using*, it will cost you less than financing the same car over a similar term (time period). However you will find that a 36 to 48 month lease will provide a similar payment to an 84 month finance loan. Consumers often feel that they would rather "own" the vehicle (so they are attracted to the financing option) rather than "rent" the vehicle under a lease option. If you are leaning in that direction, consider what financing means for you.

Here's what I mean. <u>Low financing rates</u> offered by manufacturers in recent years for extended terms (up to 84 months) <u>have seduced many consumers</u> into buying cars that would otherwise be out of their reach. If your intention is to keep the car for ten years, this strategy can have some logic but how many people's circumstances remain the same for 8 to 10 years? Once you are into that long term commitment, you had better hope that you do not get into a major accident (automatically lowers the car's trade-in value), or experience a major change in your family situation (e.g., all of a sudden you're in the wrong car for your situation), or experience a major component breakdown just beyond the warranty period (which makes the case for extended warranty coverage to match your extended financing).

According to **Edmunds.com**, *maintenance costs in years 4, 5, and 6 average $100 to $150 per month for a mid-sized sedan*. Most manufacturers' standard comprehensive warranty programs run for 3 years or 60,000 km which matches the most common lease terms and mileage. If you keep leasing, you'll always have a monthly payment but you avoid major repair bills indefinitely.

A NEW WAY TO BUY A CAR – 2ND EDITION

The critical question if you are considering a lease is <u>the difference in your position at trade-in time</u>! Let's assume you are a high mileage driver. (That is usually the argument for not leasing). On a <u>lease</u>, most manufacturers charge an excess mileage penalty of 10 cents per km. On a standard 36 month lease with a 72,000 kilometer mileage allowance (that's 24,000 km per year), adding 40,000 extra km x $0.10 costs an extra $4,000. If you have two 3-year-old cars (one at 72,000 km and another at 112,000 km), how much lower will the appraisal on the higher mileage car be? Think about it. There will be more than a $4,000 price difference if you put each up for sale. That's why it looks like leasing makes sense for the low mileage and the high mileage driver!

Some of those who are new to leasing worry about wear and tear charges at the end of the lease. Normal wear and tear will usually be waived by the manufacturer if you are planning to lease another vehicle from the same brand. If you are concerned that you will get hit by an unexpected bill at the lease-end, it is now common for car companies to hire third party inspectors and estimators so neither the manufacturer nor the dealer has an inherent conflict of interest. If you are still worried, the manufacturer offers (and would prefer you take) **lease-end protection**. For a charge (that you can roll into your payment), you can return your leased vehicle without the worry of extra charges (as long as damages do not exceed about $7,500 - varies by manufacturer). <u>If you are leasing, I recommend getting lease-end protection</u>.

Before you get hypnotized by that low 84-month financing payment, consider if leasing might make sense for you. Leasing is back and you owe it to yourself to consider this financing option when you are shopping for your next car. With the rapid changes in vehicle technologies (safety systems and fuel economy systems), buying a car is becoming less attractive when you consider that within four years, the car that you buy may be obsolete (in terms of fuel economy, active safety systems, and connectivity technologies that make your life easier). Leasing gives you the opportunity to always be driving under warranty and in a relatively new vehicle.

Chapter 8

UNDERSTANDING THE CAR BUYING PROCESS

The Importance of Value and Price

Not all Makes and Models in the same vehicle category are created equal. Similarly equipped Honda Civic, Toyota Corolla, Mazda3, Volkswagen Jetta, Ford Focus and Hyundai Elantra vehicles will be priced about the same and the incentives, over time, will be similar, however the safety systems are not equal, the crash test results will be different, the driving dynamics will be different, the future resale value will be different, the cost to insure will be different, the styling will be different, driver ergonomics will be different, and the fuel economy will be different. So, **if the price of each vehicle is the same, what are you going to do to make a decision?** In other words, <u>what characteristics do you value most</u>?

Think about what is most important to you before venturing off to the dealership so you can evaluate the vehicles you test drive based on the important criteria that you have already set. For each of the Makes and Models mentioned above, there are hundreds of thousands of people driving those vehicles who are very happy with what their vehicle does for them. Baskin-Robbins ice cream comes in 31 flavours for the same reason. **Each car brand has a design language and/or driving characteristics that will either suit you or annoy you**. For a given car Model, you may ignore the poor gas mileage because the acceleration is so good, or vice versa. Therefore, if you were evaluating the above list of vehicles (and the price were the same for each), you would value them differently from one another and your valuations would be different than mine. My point is that you will probably be spending a lot of time in your car over a number of years so you want to find one that has a "personality" that connects with yours. That's where the point of maximum value will be found.

Steps to the Sale/Purchase

The sales process that I talked about earlier has been around for a long time and includes the following steps in roughly this order. It is the goal of the salesperson to move you through this process so, by the end of the process, you are "conditioned" to say "Yes" to buying a car today. Here are the steps that all salespeople are taught and that you can expect to experience:

Meet & Greet. The object here is to build rapport and move you from cautious to accepting because the dealership knows that <u>people buy from people they know, like, and trust</u> so this is the beginning of building that relationship. If it's genuine, that's a bonus.

Qualify & Counsel. The more the salesperson knows about your (transportation) situation and other things going on in your life, the better he/she is able to select a vehicle that fits your needs and your budget. You may have a particular vehicle in mind but, based on this conversation, <u>there way be other vehicles that would work for you</u>. (This is particularly true when dealing with Used Cars where every dealership lot has a unique assortment of vehicles).

Vehicle Selection. The salesperson will want to land you on a specific vehicle to <u>focus the discussion</u> since trying to consider three or four vehicles at once is a recipe for indecision. It is probably in both your interests to fix on one vehicle at this point to simplify things and focus the conversation. You can always go back to consider other vehicles if the selected vehicle does not turn out to be the best fit.

Vehicle Presentation. Here is the salesperson's opportunity to "pitch" the selected vehicle and talk about the features, benefits, and advantages <u>important to you</u> (discerned from the Qualify stage). This is where the good salesperson will build excitement and involve you in the presentation so you start moving toward "mental ownership".

Vehicle Demonstration. The best way to find out about the vehicle is to test drive it. This is where your emotions are stimulated and you start to "connect" with the vehicle (assuming it is the right vehicle for you). If you are working with a professional, this will be a "real" test drive to fully explore the vehicle's capabilities. Beware of the salesperson who wants to only take you around the block.

Transition. As you return to the dealership, the salesperson will try to gauge your interest level and readiness to proceed by asking questions that move you toward a ***commitment***. This is also the point where your trade-in vehicle (if you have one) will be checked and discussed (if it was not done earlier in the process). This is where you will get a <u>trial close</u> such as "So, if we can get the numbers to work out, are you prepared to move ahead today?"

Facility Tour. For many customers, the vehicle is only part of the transaction, so the salesperson's job is to sell the whole package of benefits (of doing business with this dealership and this salesperson). The facility tour, including introductions to some of the people you will be dealing with, is part of offering more than just a car and a price. Once you start to see this as a long-term relationship with the dealership and its staff, you are much closer to agreeing to buy the car (that the test drive demonstrated was the perfect solution to your transportation problem).

Trial Close – Commitment. This is the point where the salesperson must determine if you are willing to commit to buying the car if any concerns or "objections' you have raised can be dealt with. For the salesperson, there is no point in providing you with a detailed proposal(s), if it is clear you are not prepared to make a decision. The reason is quite simple; the dealership can only assume that your intention is to take their proposal and "shop it" around town to see if a better deal is possible. This is why it does not help your negotiating position to say you want to think about it or that you indeed plan to continue shopping. Most dealerships will not make a proposal unless they feel there is a reasonable possibility you will accept it.

Proposal. The dealership will put together two or three proposals based on what they can afford and based on what they believe you are willing to pay. These will normally take the form of monthly payments under a couple of different scenarios such as different terms, down payments, or lease versus buy options. They should line up with what the salesperson has been able to discover about your budget and other requirements.

Close the Sale. Once you have a proposal in front of you and the vehicle meets or exceeds your requirements, the next step is to make a counter-proposal. Never accept the dealership's initial proposal. If you are reasonable, it will likely be accepted.

Invoice Services and How to Use Them Wisely

The best way to save money and know exactly what kind of a deal you are getting is to use an Invoice Service which makes it possible to cut through most of the confusion and complexities that have traditionally been part of working a great car deal. If you know what the dealer paid for the car you are considering, it should make it easier to come to terms that you consider fair.

In <u>Canada</u>, you can subscribe to the following services to obtain dealer cost information (along with any special factory rebates, allowances, or incentives) for the specific vehicle you are considering:

- **CarCostCanada** (www.CarCostCanada.com) is a subsidiary of Armada Insurance and provides up to five reports for $39.95. The information is accurate although it requires some familiarity with the vehicle(s) under consideration to determine the dealer's cost. Most dealers will ask you to pay 3% to 4% above the dealer cost if you arrive with a CCC report but you will still qualify for any/all incentives that the manufacturer has made available to regular customers.

- **Unhaggle** (www.unhaggle.com) has two services available. You can secure a report on a vehicle (just like CarCostCanada), however, the service is free. Dealers who have signed up with Unhaggle pay for your contact information when you pull a report and will be sure to be contacting you right away. One of the reasons to go with Unhaggle is because they have pre-screened dealerships by brand and region so you will be directed to a dealership that has met Unhaggle's standards for transparency and customer service quality. (Of course, you can take the information and work with any dealer). Unhaggle also has a <u>bidding service</u> where you pay a fee (about 1% of the vehicle price) and your preferred vehicle choice will be sent to several dealers who will submit closed bids on the exact vehicle (or the closest available substitute) and you simply select the lowest bidder and go to the dealer to sign the paperwork and pick up the car.

- **Automobile Protection Association** (www.apa.ca) The APA was founded by Phil Edmonston in 1969 in Montreal and now has offices in Toronto and Vancouver, as well. Phil's book,

"Lemon-Aid", has been updated annually since 1969 and provides car buying and car ownership advice. APA has its own New Vehicle Buying Service that has been in operation for many years where they take your vehicle order and shop it around various dealers to find the best deal. The benefit is that the APA will save you time and effort. However, once you pay their fee, you may not be much further ahead than getting an Unhaggle report or CCC report and walking into a dealership with an offer of cost plus 3%. Membership in the APA costs $77. You can obtain a dealer cost report on any specific vehicle (without being a member) for $25.00.

- **Canadian Automobile Association** (www.caa.ca) If you are a member of your local CAA, you can use your membership card to get discounts from affiliate dealers, however, many (perhaps, most) dealers are not affiliate members in which case you are just another customer.

In the United States, there are similar but different invoice services that you can contact to obtain "dealer cost" information for the specific vehicle you are considering:

- **TrueCar** (www.TrueCar.com) uses "certified" dealers and provides the following information for the vehicle you specified in your geographic area: Market Price (Average Paid), Factory Invoice, and MSRP (Sticker Price). You may not be getting the information needed to determine if you are getting the best available deal but the information will help determine if you are getting a fair deal. You should note that other car buying services are powered by TrueCar so the same comments apply to them. Among the firms partnered with TrueCar are USAA, Sam's Club, Consumer Reports, AAA, American Express, Geico and Farmers.

- **Edmunds** (Edmunds.com) You can use Edmunds.com to get the MSRP (Manufacturer's Suggested Retail Price) as well as the average price paid for a specific vehicle in your Zip Code which is an easy and low cost way to determine what would be a fair deal but you still won't know if it's the best available deal. Edmunds also has a "Price Promise" program that provides a confirmed price quote from a dealer in your area on a specific vehicle requested.

- **Cars Direct** (www.CarsDirect.com) will act as a broker to negotiate on your behalf for the specific vehicle you want in your Zip Code or they will direct you to the Internet Manager at a dealer in your area along with price guidance that you can use for a hassle- free purchase.
- **Kelley Blue Book** (www.kbb.com) provides what they call "Fair Purchase Price" on any vehicle you select in your Zip Code. It is not clear how they determine this price, however it is better than the MSRP but higher than the Dealer Invoice Price.

If you are buying a car in Canada, it is a complete waste of time to use a U.S. based service to determine a fair price because the pricing structure, the legislation governing vehicle sales, and the way the vehicle trims and packages are set up are often completely different from one country to another. And, if you are trying to figure out what the dealer's true cost is, the difference in terminology (between Canada and the U.S.) will make the exercise even more confusing. In the U.S., the "Invoice Price" does not refer to the actual cost paid by the dealer. That's why it is possible (in the U.S.) to buy a car at "below invoice" (because various manufacturer "hold backs" are not on the invoice but can be determined). In Canada, the "dealer net price" is the actual price that the dealer paid for the vehicle. However dealers who meet and exceed manufacturer sales targets and customer satisfaction rating goals often receive performance bonuses which are calculated and/or paid monthly, quarterly, and annually.

What Fees Must I Pay on a New Car?

Soon after I got into the car business, I started writing a blog that attempted to answer the most common questions I received from customers visiting the dealership. The most popular post was one with the same title as this section. Everyone wants to know what they will be asked to pay for the vehicle and they expect an explanation of the various charges on the purchase agreement. If you are suspicious that you will be asked to pay some phony fees, it's because that's what is common practice in the industry. Let's go over what you can expect before we consider how you can prevent being hit by phony charges.

- **The MSRP (Manufacturer's Suggested Retail Price)** is normally readily available on the manufacturer's website for every Model, Trim level, and Package. Most manufacturers have country-specific websites. Google your preferred brand and head for the local website where you will find a Shopping Tools page with a Build & Price tab. Once you are on the brand site (such as Nissan, the "Make"), select the Model (such as Rogue), then the Trim Level (such a SV-FWD) plus the SV package you want (such as the Premium Package). At the time of writing, in the USA, the 2018 Nissan Rogue SV-FWD had an MSRP of **$26,020** and the Premium Package was an additional **$1,490** for a **Total MSRP of $27,510**. In addition, you will find a Destination & Handling charge of **$975**.
- **The Destination and Handling Charge** includes a Freight component (representing the amount charged by the manufacturer to transport the vehicle from the factory to the dealer's lot) and Pre-Delivery Expense to cover the amount that the manufacturer has allowed the dealer to charge for setting up the vehicle for delivery (including all pre-delivery inspections, mechanical setups, gas fill up, and detailing). So (keeping with the Nissan Rogue example) your total is $27,510 + $975 =

$28,485 plus state and local taxes and licensing charges. In many states, you will encounter a **Doc Fee** (to cover the cost of preparing all the relevant documents). More about that shortly.

In <u>Ontario</u> Canada, where I am licensed to sell cars, there are a number of additional government mandated fees that I will cover here. The other fees and taxes that <u>must be paid in Ontario for a new car</u> are:

1. **Air Tax**. The federal government charges an air conditioner excise tax of $100 (if your vehicle has air conditioning).

2. **OTS Fee**. <u>The Ontario Tire Stewardship fee</u> is charged on all tires to cover the eventual disposal cost for the tires on your car. The government used to charge this only when you disposed of old tires but decided it was better to get the money upfront. For passenger vehicles and light trucks, the fee is currently $3.30 per tire. With four tires and a spare on your new car, the fee worked out to be $16.50 as of May 1, 2017.

3. **Gas Tax**. The Ontario Government used to collect a gas consumption tax which was eliminated when the RST (Retail Sales Tax) was replaced by the HST (Harmonized Sales Tax). Don't let a new car dealer charge you for gas. Most manufacturers require the dealer to sell the vehicle with a full tank of gas included in the price. (For Used Cars, it is common for dealers to charge for a full tank of gas).

4. **OMVIC Fee. The Ontario Motor Vehicle Industry Council** is the governing body for car dealerships and car salespeople in Ontario. OMVIC collects a $10 transaction fee to support its dispute resolution activities and policing functions. Some other provinces have similar governing bodies to police the retail auto industry to ensure best ethical practices are maintained.

5. **PPSA Fee**. If you finance or lease a vehicle, the bank or leasing company will charge a fee to set up the loan and register the lien on the vehicle under the requirements of the <u>Personal Property Security Act</u> (PPSA). This fee is usually between $75 and $150 depending on the amount and the term

of the loan. If you pay cash, this charge does not apply. Your country may have a similar charge as part of the leasing or financing set up.

6. **Licensing**. Many dealerships charge a fee to take care of the licensing of the new vehicle including transferring plates if necessary. This may be part of the dealership's Doc Fee (as described later in this section).

7. **HST**. In Canada, most goods and services are subject to a Value-Added Tax. In Ontario, the 13% HST (Harmonized Sales Tax) covers federal and provincial sales taxes. If you are trading in a vehicle, you only pay HST on the difference between the new car price and the value of your trade-in. (Most provinces and states have a sales tax that applies to the sale of motor vehicles and operates in the same manner as the Ontario example just illustrated).

The above fees and taxes are all mandatory and are not subject to negotiation. Dealers, however, often provide other additional products and/or services that are designed to increase the profit on the vehicle being sold. On these items, you can choose to purchase these extras as offered or negotiate to get the price reduced or eliminate them altogether.

Security (Etching) Package. Most dealers etch their vehicles with a police traceable code that is part of an insurance policy in case the vehicle gets stolen. You may purchase this protection, however, depending on your current automobile insurance policy, you may already have equivalent coverage from your insurance company. Look for this on your purchase agreement; it may have already been included in the payment quoted. It may be called an "Administration Charge" or it might be one of a number of charges. Always make sure that all charges are disclosed and explained before signing the Purchase Agreement.

Nitrogen Filled Tires. There are some benefits to having your tires filled with 100% nitrogen as it helps maintain constant tire pressure and helps improve tire life. If you buy it, see that you get some kind of road hazard tire warranty with it. Also note what is charged for this extra. Some dealers include it with the security/etching package.

Wheel Locks. Many cars now come with expensive alloy wheels so most dealers install wheel locks on the vehicle when it arrives on the lot. This is pretty inexpensive insurance against getting these stolen off your vehicle. Dealers usually charge about $75 to install these locks and will normally include this charge automatically on your purchase agreement. They may package wheel locks with other "security" items so ask what all "packages" include and determine if they represent good value. (They are usually overpriced).

Doc Fees or Documentation Fees. These can run from $100 to $500. They are negotiable but the dealer will tell you they are not. Some States allow dealers to charge these documentation fees up to various maximums although many States have no maximums. In most jurisdictions in Canada and the US, it is illegal to charge a Doc Fee unless it is fully disclosed in the purchase agreement.

There are lots of other products and services that dealers will offer you once you have agreed to purchase a new car. These include rust protection, extended warranty protection, life and disability insurance, loss of employment insurance, tinted windows, and various dealer installed accessories. Always scrutinize these added products or services to determine if the price charged represents good value. (These topics are covered in greater depth in *Chapter 7 - How to Win the Battle with the Business Office*).

What is Digital Car Buying? Is It the Solution?

The way that automobiles get sold is now being disrupted by brands such as Tesla, Porche, and Genesis that are adapting a purchasing model already in use by brands such as Apple and Amazon. These car brands have merged the shopping mall storefronts and online merchandising solutions in a way that has attracted and engaged shoppers. The recent launch of the Genesis brand of luxury vehicles by Hyundai has changed the game and set a new standard for automotive retail.

The traditional sales and service model that the auto industry has operated for over 100 years is overdue for disruption and digital technology (prompted by a more demanding and sophisticated buyer). In the US and Canada, you can now buy a new Genesis vehicle completely online and have it delivered to your driveway. You can have your trade-in evaluated, your financing arranged and purchase any accessories, extended warranties, or dealership services while sitting at home on your computer or tablet. Even more important, you can move back and forth between in-store and online seamlessly on your own timetable without having to repeat steps.

It is difficult to know how quickly and how completely consumers will want to adopt the "Amazon" model of car buying, however, the Genesis example appears to include a twist that addresses the freedom and flexibility that consumers seem to want. Car shoppers seem to want and expect to be able to conduct their shopping in their own way and on their own timetable. The research suggests that shoppers want to do a lot of the work online, some of the steps at the dealership, and be able to suspend their car buying project for a few days or weeks and then pick it back up again where they left off.

My own experience with thousands of online customers suggests that they prefer to have a seamless experience between researching at home and fine tuning their decision at the dealership. This means not having to go over the same ground at the dealership that they have already covered during their at-home process. **Motoinsight**, who designed the Genesis purchase platform, is one provider working with manufacturers and dealers to offer such a seamless car buying experience where every element of the car purchase process can be done online (or a mix of online and offline). With more and more car brands now moving into shopping malls and partnering with software providers that can deliver the capability and experience described above, it's likely that a major disruption is already rolling through the automotive retail sector. Some dealerships and most car manufacturers are trying to get out in front of this new way to buy a car but we are probably in for a period of dislocation as the industry struggles to change the habits and methods that have been in place for a century.

Chapter 9

UNDERSTANDING THE NEW TECHNOLOGIES FACING CAR BUYERS

Fuel Saving Technologies – A Short Primer on How to Not Be Confused

Car manufacturers are all required by international environmental agreements and national laws passed in Europe and North America to limit emissions and improve overall fuel economy in order to sell cars in these jurisdictions. Each has come up with different ways to achieve those requirements and each technology has benefits and drawbacks that consumers should be aware of as they try to select a vehicle and a technology solution.

Here are the major fuel saving technologies you will encounter and some thoughts on their benefits and drawbacks:

- **Manual Transmissions.** From a fuel savings point of view, manually shifting gears has traditionally been the most fuel efficient way to get your car moving. That's because there are fewer moving parts and less friction to deal with in a manual transmission. Doing your own shifting is now the preferred choice for driving enthusiasts who love to interact directly with the car. If you are one of these people, you will usually get a fuel savings bonus with a manual transmission. Otherwise, the vast majority of drivers in North America will be considering an automatic transmission as discussed below.

- **Continuously Variable Transmissions (CVT).** The CVT became a popular fuel saving solution about 15 years ago when Nissan adopted the technology in a big way followed by Toyota, Honda, and others. It is now a common form of "automatic" transmission. It's inexpensive to build for the car manufacturer and helps improve gas mileage because the heavy-duty drive chain allows the engine to always be operating in the "sweet spot" for minimum fuel consumption. It is similar to having an infinite number of gears so every driving situation is covered meaning the appropriate gear ratio is always selected for every situation. The big drawback with the early generation of CVTs was the noisy and sluggish performance. That has largely been eliminated to the point where a CVT can be found in most popular-priced vehicles. If you have been driving a conventional automatic for many years, you may find that a CVT takes some getting used to, however, it helps deliver improvements in gas mileage without negatively impacting performance. Traditional automatic transmissions have also become more efficient in recent years so the fuel advantages of CVTs are no longer as significant.

- **Dual Clutch Transmissions.** With these new transmissions, you have two separate <u>automated manual gearboxes</u>, each with its own clutch, but one containing the odd gears and the other the even ones. Therefore, as you're accelerating, each gearbox readies the next gear up. Dual-clutch automatics tend to offer snappy, coordinated shifts when you're driving quickly as well as a little more driving enjoyment than a typical automatic. Because of their light-weight and low-friction operation, dual clutch systems also help to save gas but are not a drag on performance.

- **Turbo-Charged Engine**. Another way to get more power from a smaller engine is to use turbocharging as Ford has been doing on their Ford EcoBoost vehicles. This process is a combination of turbocharging and direct fuel injection that improves fuel economy without sacrificing engine power. Smaller engines use less gas so the EcoBoost solution delivers improved gas mileage without giving up performance. Improvements in turbocharging technology have helped eliminate the "turbo lag" experienced in the first turbo vehicles so this earlier annoyance is less of an issue of late.

- **SKYACTIV**. Mazda's SKYACTIV solution uses direct fuel injection along with a high compression engine (instead of turbocharging) to generate increased horsepower and torque from smaller engines. It also combines the high compression engine with a dual clutch transmission and lightweight unibody structure to reduce weight which all combine to generate close-to-hybrid gas mileage but improved handling and overall performance. The next generation of SKYACTIV is a new high compression engine that Mazda is introducing that operates like a diesel, i.e., no spark plugs - called SKYACTIV-X Compression-Ignition Gas Engine. Spark Plug Controlled Compression Ignition (SPCCI) enables the SKYACTIV-X to use extremely lean fuel mixtures that can't be combusted via spark, only by compression. In late 2018, Mazda is launching the commercial version of this concept called Homogeneous Charge Compression Ignition (HCCI) technology. HCCI is a form of internal combustion in which well-mixed fuel and air are compressed to the point of auto-ignition. As in other forms of combustion, this releases considerable energy. HCCI combines characteristics of conventional gasoline and diesel engines. Mazda is promising 30% better fuel efficiency by using pressure, not spark plugs, to ignite fuel.

- **Diesel**. Vehicles that run on diesel fuel are a choice for good fuel economy with the added benefit that they provide lots of torque. Diesel fuel prices are similar to those of gasoline in North America, meaning you will save some money at the pump, however, diesel vehicles will normally cost you a couple of thousand dollars more to own. In Canada, only Chevrolet, Dodge, Mercedes, Audi, BMW, Mazda and Volkswagen currently offer diesel passenger vehicles. Since the Volkswagen scandal earlier this decade that indicated that reported fuel economy numbers were considerably overstated by VW for their diesel vehicles, it is difficult to know exactly where diesel falls on the fuel efficiency spectrum. With the maintenance costs and environment issues surrounding diesel, we may be seeing this technology becoming simply a performance enhancing technology rather than a fuel economy technology.

- **Hydrogen Fuel Cell**. A potential for the future, this zero-emissions technology promises to cut driving costs drastically, however, the lack of hydrogen filling station infrastructure means this solution is still a long shot (in my opinion). With the recent acceleration of hybrid-electric and fully-electric vehicles development and infrastructure development, it looks like Hydrogen Fuel Cell vehicles may have missed their window of opportunity even though this technology is still a viable option for other commercial (non-transportation) applications.

- **Hybrid-Electric Vehicles**. The solution that many car companies first found easiest to develop to meet strict mileage standards was the hybrid vehicle which involves downsizing the gasoline engine and adding an electric motor and battery packs. The electric motor "assists" the gasoline engine so performance is not too severely compromised, however, in the early stages, the added weight of the batteries and the somewhat sluggish acceleration resulted in a vehicle that was heavy and had mediocre handling characteristics. With recent improvements in battery technologies, hybrids are no longer much more expensive than conventional vehicles and do not suffer the same performance deficiencies. Unfortunately, (for hybrids) the great leap forward in electric battery technologies has extended the range of fully electric vehicles while the government incentives that used to flow to hybrids are now being channeled almost exclusively to fully electric vehicles meaning the net price difference is no longer as great. Some recent studies are showing that the total cost of operating a hybrid-electric vehicle is more than a fully-electric vehicle. With the gap in range dropping, hybrid-electric vehicles are becoming less attractive than fully-electric.

- **Fully Electric**. Electric Vehicles (E.V.) are not new. By 1900, 28% of vehicles produced in the U.S. were powered by electricity. Now, they are making a comeback (although with government subsidy help). Their high cost and limited range restricted their popularity, however the rapid advancements in battery technologies (along with the arrival of Elon Musk and the Tesla) is changing the game quickly and dramatically. For a detailed discussion of fully-electric vehicles, see the next item titled *"Is It Time to Get Serious About an Electric Vehicle?"*

Is It Time to Get Serious About an Electric Vehicle?

The latest generation of electric vehicles is much improved over the previous crop of EVs so any preconceived notions you have about this transportation option might be in for a reality check. I know that I have significantly adjusted my view on EVs after recently test driving a few and after talking with about a dozen different EV owners.

Let's define some terms and then discuss my recent EV experience:

- **Fully Electric** cars are powered 100% by an electric motor and battery. Fully electric cars do not burn gasoline or diesel and have zero-tailpipe-emissions. Most fully electric cars can travel 200-250 km (125-150 miles) on a full charge, with some models capable of 400+ km (250+ miles). This is the category of vehicles where all the industry research and government incentives are being directed. Fully electric vehicles look like they are the future.

- **Plug-in Hybrids** use electricity and gasoline. They can travel 20-80 km (15-50 miles), depending on model, on a full charge. Once the battery is used up, a gasoline engine or generator turns on for an additional 500+ km (300+ miles) of gasoline range. Plug-in Hybrids can do everything gas cars can do with the added benefit of providing all-electric driving for most day-to-day needs. Hybrids are a less elegant solution to the environmental issues that fully electric vehicles seem close to solving. In recent "cost of ownership" studies, hybrids come out as expensive or slightly more expensive than conventional gasoline and diesel vehicles.

I live in Ontario (Canada), where the government has been supporting the development of electric vehicles with significant incentives and building out the re-charging infrastructure to support EVs for almost a decade. It seems like the sudden explosion of new EV models onto the market is coinciding with the building of the infrastructure to support this new vehicle technology. Over the past year, I have been talking to a variety of people on the front lines of the EV phenomenon to discover whether this is a viable option for car buyers. As a driving enthusiast, I must admit entering the initial conversations with EV owners with a bias against EVs. It seemed to me that an electric vehicle weighed down with heavy batteries could not provide a quick and nimble fun-to-drive experience. And those are the characteristics I find most attractive in a car. Let me share what my research and what talking to numerous EV owners revealed.

One of the EV owners I interviewed is a professor at a local college. He talked to me about his experience leasing a Nissan LEAF (100% EV) over the past three years. He uses the LEAF to commute and, even though he has a gas-powered SUV as well, he looks for every opportunity to drive his LEAF because the idea of stopping at a gas station has become a rather distasteful activity for him and his family. He will be renewing his lease this year (as Nissan launches a fully re-designed LEAF for 2018) and here's why:

- He spends about $30 per month on electricity to power his LEAF versus $175+ to do the same driving in an equivalent gas powered vehicle.
- There is effectively no maintenance on the LEAF, i.e., no gas (of course), no oil changes, and very little brake wear as the regenerative braking system means taking your foot off the "gas" pedal will bring the vehicle to a virtual stop without applying the brakes. Brakes only come into play if you need to stop quickly.
- His Nissan LEAF (and this is a characteristic of all EVs) is great fun to drive because the electric motor develops so much torque (187 lb.ft.) that the car delivers instant and powerful acceleration. By comparison, most compact gas-powered cars develop 25% less than that. As someone who highly values the "fun to drive" aspect of any car, I was truly impressed by the

various electric vehicles I test drove. They all were responsive and had that "kick" on acceleration that is addictive if you are a driving enthusiast.

- Cost of ownership. The price of fully electric vehicles is still higher than a similar sized gas-powered vehicle, however, government incentives (depending on where you live) as well as the fuel and maintenance savings are tipping the balance to make EVs very competitive. When you consider the total cost of ownership including fuel and routine maintenance costs, EVs are starting to look better than even the most fuel efficient gas-powered vehicles.

- In the past, the distance that EVs could travel without a charge has been an issue as the charging station infrastructure is still being built (there are now over 7,000 charging stations in Canada according to CAA and over 16,500 in the US according to statista.com) so there seems to be a critical mass developing that makes most commuting and long trips very practical. With navigation systems onboard EVs, you plug in your destination and the EV tells you where (and if) you may need to stop for a charge and selects the most efficient route.

Despite these personal experience stories, I was still feeling a bit of "range anxiety" (as they call it in the EV world). However, the latest generation of EVs is now capable of travelling between 200 km and 500 km (125 - 300 miles) on a single charge (with Tesla occupying the longest range honours). The new 2018 Nissan LEAF, for example, has a stated average range of up to 300 km (about 200 miles) so if you consider that most people have a daily commute well below those figures, plugging in at home overnight should cover most daily driving activity. Some Plug-in Hybrids, like the BMW i3 that I drove at the AutoShow have a "range extender" in the form of a 9L gas tank connected to a 2 cylinder motorcycle engine that will extend the 183 km electric-only range to 240 km when the 2-cylinder gas engine kicks in.

Insurance is one of the costs of owning a motor vehicle and because the costs to repair electric vehicles are higher than conventional vehicles, you may find your insurance bill is higher. A recent study (2015) in California found EV insurance costs were about 20% higher. In other jurisdictions, insurance companies appear to be taking a cautious approach until they have a better handle on the risks. As more EVs get on the road, it's likely that insurance companies will have more data to bring rates into line with conventional vehicles. However, a recent study by NerdWallet concluded that the overall 5-year cost of ownership was as much as 36% lower for an electric vehicle.

So, if we have arrived at lower overall ownership costs for electric vehicles over conventional gas-powered cars and the next generation of longer range electric vehicles with improved battery technologies are now being introduced, this could well be the inflection point we have been looking for. As long as the government incentives remain in place, we could be in for a major disruption in the auto industry. And it may be imminent.

A great place for unbiased information on electric vehicles is **Plug'n Drive** which is a non-profit organization committed to accelerating the adoption of electric vehicles to maximize their environmental and economic benefits. Since 2011, **Plug'n Drive** has established itself as a leader in the electric vehicle industry. It should be considered a trusted source of unbiased information about electric cars, charging stations and the electricity sector. They have recently opened an *EV Discovery Centre in Toronto* where you can test drive the latest electric vehicle models from leading manufacturers. It's a great concept because you can learn all about this new category of vehicles in a relaxed environment without getting a sales pitch (other than the unbridled enthusiasm of the folks at **Plug'n Drive** for whom electric vehicles is part of a greater environmental mission).

Making Sense of the New Active Safety Technologies

Almost all car manufacturers around the world are <u>setting the stage for fully autonomous cars.</u> Most manufacturers have committed to having the capability embedded in their vehicles by Model Year 2020 and most are targeting to be able to "flip the switch" to automated driving by Model Year 2022. In the meantime, these technologies will continue to be perfected and tested. You will see more of these technologies available on even entry-level vehicles within the next few years.

Before we get ahead of ourselves, most manufacturers are not attempting to take the driver out of driving. However, they are pushing ahead on technologies that seek to make the automobile an extension of the driver. In other words, if **cars can be made to avoid and mitigate collisions while leaving the driver in control**, that would be a great benefit to driving enthusiasts as well as those who consider cars as merely a transportation option. With the latest advances in digital technology and machine learning, it is possible to do that but also for the car to "know" when the driver is no longer in control (and therefore about to experience a crash). This is the point where the vehicle takes over and applies the brakes to avoid or minimize a near certain collision.

These capabilities are made possible by hundreds of **sensors that are communicating information about the vehicle's environment** (hundreds of times per second). For example, your vehicle now knows if it is snowing or raining, whether you are going up or down a hill, and what distance it would take to stop under the current conditions. How? It's sensors know if it is driving on an incline. The temperature gauge and the rain-sensing wipers know that the precipitation is probably snow because the temperature is a couple of degrees below freezing and the traction control system is determining the slipperiness of the road surface. It is also noting how all these elements are changing as you drive and is making "just-in-case" calculations. If the object ahead of the vehicle is getting relatively closer, your car can determine when and if it should apply the brakes to avoid a collision. If you have your foot on the accelerator pedal (the car can sense that), it "knows" you are not aware of the looming danger.

Advances in software sophistication and computing power mean that a lot of different systems can work together to keep you safe. For example, the early All Wheel Drive (AWD) systems were relatively mechanical and standalone in nature, and reactive rather than adaptive. If the front wheels were slipping, the system would react and a portion of the power would be transferred to the rear wheels. By contrast, today, the vehicle understands the outside conditions and can start engaging the AWD system as conditions change, and even anticipate conditions so the AWD system is already engaged when it is needed to negotiate a slippery corner or provide greater steering control. This is what manufacturers' advertising means when it refers to **Adaptive or Predictive AWD**.

Every car manufacturer uses slightly different terminology to describe the same safety technologies but the two major categories are **Passive Safety Devices** and **Active Safety Devices**. The term Active Safety is used to refer to technology <u>assisting in the prevention of a crash</u> and Passive Safety refers to components of the vehicle (primarily airbags, seatbelts and the physical structure of the vehicle) that help to <u>protect occupants during a crash</u>. Here is a short review and explanation of each Passive and Active Safety technology you are likely to encounter during your car purchase project:

Passive Safety Systems Now Standard on Most Vehicles.

- **Tire Pressure Monitoring Systems** (TPMS) monitor tire pressures in all four tires and warn of imbalances that may affect handling dynamics and tire wear.

- **Traction Control Systems** (TCS) restore traction if drive wheels begin to spin by using the **Anti-lock Braking System** (ABS) and **Electronic Stability Control** (ESC) in combination.

  o Electronic Stability Control intervenes to avert an impending loss of control usually on slippery surfaces. The ESC system will help keep the vehicle from skidding out of control on a curve.

  o Anti-lock Braking Systems (ABS) maintain steering control during panic braking situations by keeping the wheels turning (by pulsating the brakes very rapidly) and helping to stop on slippery surfaces.

- **Electronic Brake Force Distribution** systems (EBFD) operate the front and rear brakes independently to maintain controlled braking regardless of the weight distribution within the vehicle.

- **Emergency Brake Assist** systems (often called Emergency Forward Braking) detect panic braking behaviour and automatically apply maximum braking force while using the EBFD system to keep the vehicle level and under control.

- **Adaptive Headlamps** control the direction and range of the headlight beams to light the driver's way through curves and maximize seeing distance without partially blinding other drivers. Adaptive headlamps point the headlights towards the left or right as the steering wheel is turned.

- **Rain Sensing Wipers** use a sensor in the windshield to sense rain and engage the wipers automatically. It's a safety feature when water and slush thrown on to the windshield would otherwise temporarily blind the driver. Rain-sensing wipers can engage to clear the windshield quicker than the driver can react.

- **Parking Sensors** in the front and/or rear bumper signal to the driver how close the vehicle is getting to the vehicle ahead or behind by chirping faster as the vehicle gets closer.

- **SurroundView (AroundView) Monitor** systems use four cameras (front, rear, and one under each outside mirror) to assemble a 360 degree view of the outside of the vehicle. These systems are usually combined with sonar sensors that also detect movement in the vicinity of the vehicle.

Crash Avoidance & Driver Assistance (Active Safety Systems)

These are systems to help the driver to detect obstacles and to control the vehicle. For example, **Automatic Braking** systems engage when a collision appears certain, to prevent or reduce the severity of the collision. Some come with a warning system as well. A backup camera is now required in most jurisdictions and is often combined with a **Rear Cross Traffic Alert** system to warn of vehicles approaching from the left or right while you are backing out of your driveway or out of a shopping mall parking space. And, if you never really mastered parallel parking on a downtown city street, many vehicles now offer an automated (hands-free) parking system.

When you are out on the road (especially the highway), a whole series of safety aids are available to assist you and cover for lapses in attention that can happen to anyone. One of these is **Adaptive Cruise Control** (ACC) which is an "intelligent" cruise control system that can be used on city streets and roads as well as on major highways. ACC uses radar to maintain a safe distance from the vehicle in front. This is one of the elements of the coming self-driving car. Another element is **Lane Departure Warning** (LDW) which alerts the driver of an unintended departure from the lane of travel. Some vehicles now also include a feature that gently "nudges" the vehicle back into its intended lane if it should start to wander across the line. Nissan has recently combined ACC and LDW in its **ProPILOT Assist** which will keep you in your current lane (nudging you back on track if you wander) and will adjust your speed to keep you a safe distance from the vehicle ahead. It will do this at any speed down to a full stop so it works on open road highway driving as well as stop-and-go city driving. It is pretty much single lane self-driving although it warns you if your hands are not on the steering wheel.

With the popularity of SUVs as the new "family car", one of the most popular safety features in recent years is **Blind Spot Monitoring (BSM)** normally available with **Rear Cross Traffic Alert (RCTA)**. All SUVs are characterized by blind spots to the left rear and right rear corners of the vehicle. On the highway, a portion of the adjacent lane (left and right) toward the rear of the vehicle is normally the blind spot. With BSM, radar in the rear bumper monitors the area beside and to the rear of your SUV and provides a visual warning when a vehicle enters that zone. If you use your turn signal to change lanes, you will get an immediate warning sound. The same system operates when you are backing out of a parking spot to alert you to traffic approaching from either direction. The popularity of these latter features (along with a backup camera) has resulted in most SUV manufacturers making BSM and RCTA standard on even their entry level SUVs. (These features are now standard on many mid-sized sedans as well).

GORDON N. WRIGHT

Pedestrian Detection and Injury Avoidance & Mitigation

It's great that we now have a set of technologies that help prevent colliding with other vehicles but where are we when it comes to avoiding pedestrians? The next wave of collision avoidance capabilities is already dealing with pedestrians. It's also worth considering that the move toward fully autonomous vehicles requires the ability for vehicles to avoid hitting pedestrians. This has already become an issue with electric vehicles in particular since pedestrians cannot hear them coming. Also, until recently, the software that can distinguish between a pedestrian and a pole has not been available. But now, software than can distinguish between a moving person and any other moving object is a reality.

These systems work by using stereoscopic cameras mounted behind the rearview mirror and radar in the front grill which provide an effective way of detecting the more subtle movements of people. These systems are more effective at slower speeds. So far, pedestrian detection may not always be able to help avoid a collision, but this feature can help reduce the speed enough to make the impact more survivable. As research progresses, infrared technology is being added to improve performance, especially at night. Look for these pedestrian-friendly systems over the next couple of years. At the same time, manufacturers have been busy re-designing the shape of cars (especially the front end) to limit the damage done to pedestrians during a collision. Many of these design standards were originally mandated by European governments and are now part of vehicle design worldwide.

Chapter 10

WHY YOU WANT A FRIEND IN THE CAR BUSINESS

People tell me that it's great to have a friend in the car business because you want to have a friend and advisor when you're in the process of buying a car. It's not easy figuring out what transportation solutions make the most sense. After all, you're trying to juggle what you need with what you want and what you can afford. So, the job of the Product Advisor (nobody calls them sales consultants any more) at the dealership is to help you sort through those issues and select a vehicle that meets all or most of your criteria.

The best Product Advisors will steer you toward a vehicle and a method of paying for it that fits your needs and pocketbook. Your advisor (and certainly the dealership Sales Manager) should have your long term interests in mind. Getting you into the wrong vehicle is not in the long term interests of the dealership. More than ever, dealerships (and the people who work there) can only survive if they are basing their strategy on the <u>lifetime value of each customer</u>. The "one and done" selling strategy is being rejected by more and more dealerships. This trend is being forced upon dealerships by manufacturers (who cannot build a brand if customers do not return for their next vehicle) and by social media where you will quickly discover those dealerships and salespeople to avoid as you research your next vehicle purchase.

As I have written about frequently since I got into the car business over a decade ago, you owe it to yourself to spend a portion of your research time discovering who to do business with. Because it is very difficult to fool Google, you can now find (and "audition") the person you want to work with on your car purchase project. You will want to be working with a Product Advisor or Sales Manager with integrity, transparency, and compassion as well as the expertise to offer real solutions to your transportation situation. With the vast array of digital tools now available to us, you can locate these people without leaving your home.

As you may have determined while reading this guide, I still work at a dealership but I now spend much of my time working with salespeople on how to build a large following of happy customers for themselves and for the dealership. At the same time, I still get to interact with customers and prospective customers daily as they search out answers about buying and owning a vehicle. This role has helped me stay tuned in to how people buy cars (using all the digital tools at their disposal) and what kind of difficulties they encounter along the way. As the industry and technology evolve, some of the hassles of buying a car continue to plague the industry while other problems get solved. For those of us who are privileged to work at dealerships with enlightened management, the objective is to provide a "dream-come-true" purchase experience by simplifying the whole process.

If there is a question that this guide has not addressed, I would encourage you to let me know so I can get you the answer. You are also invited to visit my website where you can subscribe to my newsletter and blog for helpful advice on car buying and car ownership.

Hey. Thanks again for reading. Perhaps I'll see you at the dealership.

Gordon Wright,
A Friend in the Car Business

Chapter 11

CAR BUYING RESOURCES

Most of the references in this Consumer Awareness Guide are based on buying a car in Ontario, Canada where the legislation, regulations, and consumer protections are among the most rigorous in North America. If you live in another Canadian Province or in the United States, the principles outlined in this guide still apply, however, your recourse to government agencies to assist you will be different. Here is a list of resources by province and by state as well as some topics we touched on earlier in the book:

CANADA

Prov.	Protection for Car Buyers	Vehicle Licensing Authority
BC	Motor Vehicle Sales Authority of B.C. www.mvsabc.com	Insurance Corporation of B.C. www.icbc.com
AB	Alberta Motor Vehicle Industry Council. www.amvic.org	Service Alberta. www.servicealberta.ca

SK	Saskatchewan Motor Dealers Act. www.justice.gov.sk.ca	S.G.I. www.sgi.sk.ca
MB	Manitoba Consumer Protection Office. www.gov.mb.ca/cca/cpo	Manitoba Public Insurance. http://mpi.mb.ca
ON	Ontario Motor Vehicle Industry Council. www.omvic.on.ca	Ministry of Transportation of Ontario. www.mto.gov.on.ca
QC	Consumer Protection Office. www.opc.gouv.gc.ca	S.A.A.Q. www.saaq.gouv.qc.ca/en
NB	Government of Canada Consumer Information. www.consumerinformation.ca	Service New Brunswick. www.snb.ca/e
NS	Government of Canada Consumer Information. www.consumerinformation.ca	Service Nova Scotia. www.novascotia.ca/sns/mv
PE	Government of Canada Consumer Information. www.consumerinformation.ca	Prince Edward Island Transportation & Infrastructure. www.gov.pe.ca/highwaysafety

NL	Government of Canada Consumer Information. www.consumerinformatio n.ca	Service Newfoundland. www.servicenl.gov.nl.ca
NU	Government of Canada Consumer Information. www.consumerinformatio n.ca	Government of Nunavut. www.gov.nu.ca/
NW	Government of Canada Consumer Information. www.consumerinformatio n.ca	North West Territories Depart of Transportation. dmv.dot.gov.nt.ca/vehicle-registration
YK	Government of Canada Consumer Information. www.consumerinformatio n.ca	Yukon Highways & Public Works. www.hpw.gov.yk.ca/mv/

UNITED STATES

The "one stop shop" for all questions about your car buying rights by state can be found on this non-government website: **www.dmv.org**

All state regulations and forms can be found at this single non-government website along with helpful tips. Enter your state and everything you need is easily accessible: www.dmv.org

Other Resources

Electric Vehicles:

Buyers of plug-in hybrids and electric cars in the US benefit from a tax credit of $2,500 to $7,500, depending on the size of the battery in the car and where you purchase it. In Canada, rebates on electric vehicles are as high as $14,000. Different provinces in Canada have different EV incentives.

Fully Electric Vehicles: (Currently Available in Ontario)

- smart fortwo MSRP = $29,050
- Ford Focus Electric MSRP = $34,998
- Hyundai IONIQ Electric MSRP = $35.649
- Kia Soul Electric MSRP = $35,895
- Nissan LEAF MSRP = $35,998
- Volkswagen e-Golf MSRP = $36,355
- Chevrolet VOLT MSRP - $39,095
- Chevrolet BOLT MSRP = $43,195
- BMW i3 MSRP = $48,750
- Tesla Model S MSRP = $96,650
- Tesla Model X MSRP = $110,200
- Tesla Model 3 MSRP = $45,600 (Upgrades to be available)

Most manufacturers also have Plug-in Hybrid vehicles available as part of their overall product line with government incentives that vary by jurisdiction. Plug-in Hybrids include both an electric motor for short distance driving supplemented by a conventional gasoline engine for extended range driving.

Charging Your EV or Plug-in Hybrid. To keep your vehicle charged, you will want a household charging station that is simple, smart, sturdy and safe. The most popular solution is the **FLO Home™** electric vehicle charging station for single-family homes that sells in Canada for $995. More information is available at **https://flo.ca**

Carsharing:

Carsharing Association is getting traction as new transportation systems enabled by current smartphone technology make the logistics so much easier than ever to access a vehicle on short notice. More general information can be found at **http://carsharing.org/**

The University of California, Berkeley's Transportation Sustainability Research Center (TSRC), a leading provider of independent shared-use mobility research, announced the release of its Carsharing Market Outlook. Check details at **http://www.its.berkeley.edu/node/13158**

Maven (**https://www.mavendrive.com**) is a carsharing service announced by General Motors in January 2016. It subsequently expanded to most major US cities and recently launched in Toronto. Maven makes it possible to access a GM vehicle by the hour, day, week or month. Maven is also a way to attract younger customers to the GM brand. It has been reported that millennials make up 78 percent of the app's users, with the average customer age coming in at 30 which is a demographic all car companies are eager to attract.

Among the other competitors in this space are ***Car2Go*** (a subsidiary of Daimler AG which offers Mercedes Benz vehicles for use) with no reservations required. You just leave it in designated "home areas" with no need to return it where it originated. Also, ***Enterprise CarShare*** and ***Zipcar*** are companies offering similar use-of-a-car services.

Car Purchase "Cooling Off" Period:

The "Cooling Off Period" for Vehicle Purchases varies by jurisdiction. Be careful when signing a purchase agreement as most jurisdictions do not permit you to change your mind. Here is the situation in various Provinces and States:

Canada: There is no cooling off period in Newfoundland, Nova Scotia, New Brunswick, Prince Edward Island, Ontario, Manitoba,

Saskatchewan, and Alberta. In British Columbia, there is no cooling off period for <u>cash or finance purchases</u> but there is a <u>24 hour cooling off period for leases</u>. In Quebec, you have <u>2 days</u> from signing the purchase agreement to cancel the deal unless you have taken possession of the vehicle.

United States: The Federal Trade Commission (FTC) rules generally apply to motor vehicle sales. If you are buying a Used Car, the FTC's Used Car Rule requires auto dealers to display on used cars a window sticker called a Buyers Guide with important information for consumers. For the purchase of new cars, review the regulations and articles at the following FTC landing page for more detail: https://www.consumer.ftc.gov/topics/buying-owning-car. For more specifics on Used Cars, also review https://www.consumer.ftc.gov/articles/0055-buying-used-car.

Australia: No cooling off period for new car purchases from a car dealer but used car purchases are subject to a 1-day cooling off period.

Europe: If you live in Europe and plan to purchase a motor vehicle within your own country or you plan to purchase in another EU country and register the vehicle in your home country, the regulations can be a bit complicated. Also, if you are purchasing a vehicle in Europe for export to North America or elsewhere, a good place to start your research is at https://europa.eu/european-union/index_en (the official website of the EU). More specific information on purchasing a vehicle can be found at https://europa.eu/youreurope/citizens/vehicles/cars/index_en.htm.

ABOUT THE AUTHOR

When Gordon Wright found himself downsized following a successful 25+ year career in corporate marketing and sales, he decided to try selling cars and joined the team at a local dealership. He soon discovered that the way dealerships and car salespeople were generally conducting business was a lot different than the approach he had found common in the corporate world. Having spent most of his life applying marketing principles designed to deliver customers to the front door, he was convinced that his key to success in this new environment would be to use his marketing skills and understanding of buyer behaviour to provide a different customer experience.

One of his first steps in educating car buying prospects was a blog he created called *"A Friend in the Car Business"* that acted as a "consumer awareness guide" for car buyers. This eventually turned into a book *"A New Way to Buy a Car"* published in early 2015. He also set up a YouTube channel that provided similar car buying advice and tips as well as vehicle walkaround videos on new and used cars.

Since entering the car business in 2007, he has directly helped many hundreds of car buyers discover a new way to buy a car and he has reached thousands more via his various social media platforms, monthly newsletter, and through his work at major new car dealerships in Metro Toronto. His education-based approach has won him a large and loyal following. Writing on the topic and providing advice to car buyers has always been his priority while he shares a lifelong passion for cars and driving.

Gordon's sales approach was based on the philosophy that an educated buyer is an easier customer to work with. This is how he built a large and solid base of customers who appreciated his unique style. At the same time, the internet and social media were providing more tools for car buyers to begin to level the playing field. Although changes are occurring quickly, the industry is still populated by a significant percentage of "old school" thinking in an industry with customers no longer willing to tolerate the tactics and techniques so common in the past.

So, by thinking differently, Gordon Wright pioneered a <u>New Way to Buy Cars</u> whether the activity was being conducted in the showroom or online. He realized that these methods worked better than the "old school" tactics employed by many of his colleagues, and he was rewarded with a parade of repeat customers and referrals. Educated customers, he found, were happy customers and were eager to spread the word.

Gordon Wright is a lifelong marketing and sales professional who lives near Toronto, Canada. He holds an MBA in Marketing from the Schulich School of Business at York University and a Bachelor of Business Management from Ryerson University.

www.ingramcontent.com/pod-product-compliance
Lightning Source LLC
Chambersburg PA
CBHW061149040426
42445CB00013B/1623